# Scotland's Ghosts
# and Apparitions

Terence Whitaker has had a varied career,
working in the Prison Service, the Civil
Service and the theatre, and is now a
full-time writer and broadcaster. He has
written several books on the supernatural
including *Ghosts of Old England* and
*England's Ghostly Heritage*, and has appeared
on many well-known radio and television
programmes.

# Scotland's Ghosts and Apparitions

TERENCE WHITAKER

ROBERT HALE · LONDON

ISBN 0 7090 4441 0

Robert Hale Limited
Clerkenwell House
Clerkenwell Green
London EC1R 0HT

Photoset in North Wales by
Derek Doyle & Associates, Mold, Clwyd.
Printed in Great Britain by
St Edmundsbury Press, Bury St Edmunds, Suffolk.
and bound by WBC Bookbinders Ltd, Bridgend, Glamorgan.

# Contents

For Mavis Croft,
With Love

'I must own that when the door was shut I began to consider myself as too far from the living and somewhat too near the dead.'

Sir Walter Scott – writing about his stay at
Glamis Castle

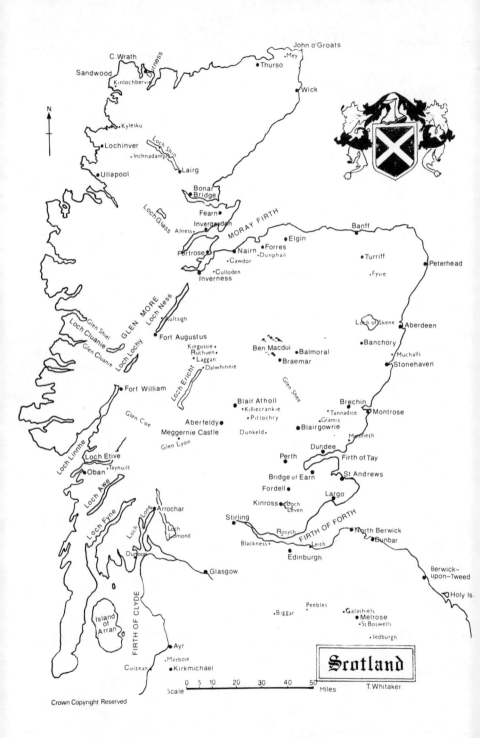

# Preface

Since the beginning of history Scotland has been two nations – the Lowlands, where some form of settled government was at least possible; and the Highlands, where the King's writ seldom ran. Each heartily disliked the other, each distrusted the other, and indeed few of the great Scottish figures whose names and deeds are remembered today in songs and folk-tales were admired by all Scotsmen in their own lifetime. Bonnie Prince Charlie was detested by the Lowland Scot, and the Highlanders were indifferent to such Lowland heroes as the Black Douglas or Kinmont Willie. And practically every Scotsman – Highlander or Lowlander – disliked Mary, Queen of Scots, whose only truly heroic trait was, in their eyes, her personal courage in the face of adversity.

The Highlander believes that the past is as real as the present. Tales of heroes and of battles long ago have been remembered for centuries. Clan feuds, the adventures of Bonnie Prince Charlie and his followers, and the tragedy of the Highland Clearances are as fresh in folk-memory as events which the story-tellers themselves have witnessed.

Sentiment and the primitive virtues of loyalty, courage and toughness are oddly mingled in the Highland character, and in the long winter nights of this harsh land people still gather for the musical evening of the ceilidh and to listen to the seannachie, or story-teller, telling and retelling stories and legends of long-forgotten events in Highland history.

The Lowlands, on the other hand, caught between the millstones of England and the tough Highlands, has been for much of its history a poor region. Indeed, it was the poverty-stricken appearance of King James I's Lowland couriers which, so we are told, gave rise to the legend of the Scots' meanness. But if the people were financially poor, they were

9

rich in pride and courage which glowed through some of the darkest moments of Scotland's past.

Admirable though these qualities are, they did not make for a peaceful nation. There *is* glory and honour in the history of the Scottish nation, but there is treachery and bloodshed too. Wars and feuds, abduction and murder were commonplace and carried out in total contempt of authority. Out of these deeds came the tales of the makkars – the poets and makers of ballads.

It will come as no surprise to learn that Scotland is rich in ghost-lore, with even the smallest village claiming some lingering traditional story of a haunted spot. Castles, manor houses, humble cottages, old inns, crossroads and rivers all have or have had their ghosts.

This book is about two types of ghost: the one in folklore which no one can actually claim to have seen; and the other more interesting but less romantic ghost which has been witnessed by and shared the daily lives of the people I have met or who have written to me.

A few of these ghosts, it would appear, have a sense of humour, but most are grim, malicious and often have no apparent reason to haunt a particular spot. Some of these stories are not particularly pleasant, dealing as they do with terrible violence, inhuman practices, lust, greed, jealousy, violated promises and sudden death. Women and children were amongst those unfortunates who were butchered in times of religious strife or political intolerance, and who have returned in many instances as ghosts.

Murderers and highwaymen were hung in chains, and witches and suicides were buried with stakes thrust through their hearts. No wonder then that the highways of Scotland are 'alive' with the violent history of the past.

As ever, a great many people of diverse ways of life have helped me to write this book. To these people I owe a great personal debt and offer my sincere thanks for their assistance.

There are some people who deserve a special mention: my wife, Marjorie, for her ever-helpful encouragement and patience; the many newspaper and magazine editors throughout Scotland who very kindly published my letters asking for ghost stories; the countless librarians and their staff for their invaluable assistance; BBC Television, Scotland;

Grampian Television; BBC Radio Scotland; Radio Clyde; BBC Highland and Radio Tay; Grantown-on-Spey Heritage Centre; Mrs Alison Berg, Kelso; Mrs Ann Davidson, Aberdeen; Mr Ewen Donaldson, Dunphail; Mr James Duggan, Glasgow; Mr Jack Geddes, Aberdeen; Mrs Christina George, Aberdeen; Mrs Annie McLennon, Fyvie; Mr Dave MacDairmaid, Grampian Transport Marketing Manager, Aberdeen; Mr Gerald Main, Milton Keynes; Mr Ewan Pidgeon, Richmond; Mrs Elizabeth Shipley, Hawick; Mrs Anne Smith, Aberdeen; the late Lt Richard Smith, RN Retd, Liverpool; Mrs Barbara Totty, Burnley and the many contributors who, reticent by nature, desired to remain anonymous, but who very kindly allowed me to use their contributions in the text.

Finally, my grateful thanks to Margaret and Alan Pidgeon, who very kindly gave of their time to check the manuscript for misspelt Scottish and Gaelic words, points of geography and historical accuracy.

Without the help of all these lovely people, the book could not have been written.

Burnley, 1990                                        Terence Whitaker

# 1 Haunted Castles

Long after the southern and central areas of Britain had lapsed into comparative peace, clan warfare still persisted in Scotland and, apart from the great Norman castles of the Middle Ages and the splendid baronial piles of the sixteenth to nineteenth centuries, castles were generally more modest.

These stark tower houses were the strongholds of the chieftains and landowners of every degree. They were often rebuilt or enlarged as the years went by to bring them into line with the mainstream of castle design, although they frequently retained signs of an earlier simplicity. Others were simply plain stone towers with halls and projecting turrets built on, to enable them to be defended against feuding clansmen or border reivers by a comparatively small number of bowmen or musketeers.

Hermitage Castle is one of the loneliest fortresses in Britain: a squat thirteenth-century castle set amidst the bleak, stark moorland, about twelve miles south of Hawick on the B6399.

This gaunt, solitary and forbidding ruin was built to watch over Liddesdale, the western gateway into Scotland. Until the middle of the sixteenth century it changed hands constantly. In 1342, Sir Alexander Ramsay was starved to death in its north-east tower, a site which has been described as 'a frightful dungeon, lightless, airless and devoid of sanitation'. In 1566 Mary, Queen of Scots, risked her life to visit Hermitage Castle, riding over from Jedburgh to see her lover, the Earl of Bothwell, who was staying here to recover from wounds gained in a fight.

One of the castle's more infamous occupants was the 'wicked' Lord Soulis. The dungeons were said to have been used by this enthusiast of the black arts for numerous horrible deeds, and local belief is that among the many horrors perpetrated by him was the murder of young children from nearby farms, who were kidnapped and kept in the same dungeon where Sir Alexander Ramsay died, until they were required for some foul ceremony or other.

Retribution caught up with him in the form of parents and relatives who banded together and stormed the castle, capturing Lord Soulis. They bound him in iron chains and a 'lead blanket' and boiled him alive in his own giant cauldron. A fitting end, no doubt, but the old castle, unable to support the load of iniquity which had accumulated within its walls, is said to have partly sunk beneath the ground.

Today, farm-workers and the occasional walker frequently report hearing horrifying screams and blood-curdling moans of tortured children coming from inside the ancient walls.

Crathes Castle stands about three miles from Banchory, on the A93 in Kincardine, and once formed the nucleus of the Barony of Leys.

Owned today by the National Trust for Scotland, the castle dates back to about 1553, when the double square tower was built in the Scottish baronial style with turrets and battlements. It was completed when the Bell family remodelled the upper parts about 1600. A three-storey wing was added in the eighteenth century, and later, a Queen Anne wing, which sadly was to be destroyed by fire in 1966.

For many years the 'Green Lady's Room' has had a reputation for being haunted and, even today, there are still occasional reports by visitors of seeing the ghost of a poor young woman whose skeleton was discovered during a period of renovation and restoration. Accompanying the skeleton were the remains of a baby, believed to be the reason behind a double murder.

Sometime in the mid-1700s, the daughter of the owner of Crathes Castle found herself pregnant after dallying with a local gillie, thus bringing disgrace on the family name. The scandal could not be kept secret unless both mother and child were to disappear from the scene and the father dismissed.

It was to be a further 150 years before the truth was uncovered and the pitiful remains were discovered, something which appears to have had no effect whatever on the frequent appearances of the 'Green Lady'. She has been seen so often over the years that she has now become accepted as a fact of life and an official tourist attraction.

Another Green Lady can be found at Muchalls Castle, which stands just off the A92 at Stonehaven.

Built around 1600, Muchalls Castle is reputed to be haunted by the ghost of a young woman, and although it has not been witnessed by people in recent years, there have been reports of a disturbing and inexplicable icy atmosphere which strikes right to the bones.

The story behind this haunting is connected with an alleged underground passage leading from the castle to the former wine store. This same passage often provided a quick getaway to the sea and was frequently used by former occupants, both for smuggling and as a means of escape. A daughter of the house had a boyfriend on one of the ships and, having sighted the vessel lying offshore, she went down the tunnel to meet him. She knew he would be rowing to the entrance of the passage, which opened out into a large tidal cave.

Unfortunately, the girl slipped on the seaweed-covered rocks, and fell into the water and drowned. Now it is her phantom – known as the Green Lady – that is said to appear in the drawing-room periodically.

There is a story told of how, earlier this century during Lord Robertson's occupation of Muchalls Castle, an incident occurred when a weekend guest arrived late. The dressing-bell had sounded and the guest was advised to hurry. He later reported that, on his way downstairs to the dining-room, he passed a bedroom door which was slightly ajar and, glancing in, saw a girl in a yellow frock looking at herself in front of the mirror.

On reaching the dining-room where the others were waiting to begin dinner, the guest was unconcerned about being late, as he was sure he was not the last to arrive. However, he was quite taken aback to learn that the lady he had described did not exist. He was told that he had just witnessed the phantom Green Lady of Muchalls Castle!

Without doubt, the most famous of all the haunted castles of Scotland is Glamis Castle in Angus. If there were a prize for the most horrific haunting of a Scottish castle, then it would surely go to the Queen Mother's family home.

Glamis is the seat of the earls of Strathmore, the birthplace of Princess Margaret, and reputed to be the most haunted house in Britain. Outwardly it does much to further this claim, with its grim-looking cluster of ancient towers and turrets in stone. Inside, too, many of the gloomy rooms, long stone-flagged corridors and cold echoing vaults with walls fifteen feet thick in places, all combine to give an overpowering air of antiquity and eeriness.

It is reputed to be the place where Macbeth murdered King Duncan in 1040. A sword and a shirt of mail, both supposedly belonging to Macbeth, are on view in one of the rooms.

The Queen Mother delights in telling the younger members of the royal family the spine-chilling tales that have sprung up around Glamis. How Lord 'Beardie' Crawford and his fellow revellers diced with the Devil in a tower room, and were condemned to stay there, eternally drinking until the Day of Judgement; and how the Ogilvies, fleeing from the Lindsays during a clan war, were locked in a room and forgotten, thus starving to death.

The Queen Mother is one of the many to have seen the Grey Lady of Glamis who haunts the clock tower. She is believed to be the spectre of Lady Janet Douglas, wife of the sixth Lord Glamis, who was burned at the stake on Castle Hill at Edinburgh in 1537, falsely accused of plotting to poison King James V.

But there is one Glamis phantom that few in the family are keen to talk about. Nineteenth-century high society was alive with rumours that a hideously deformed beast of a man had been born into the Strathmore clan; an incredibly strong, hairy, odd-shapen creature whose head ran straight into a huge body supported on stick-like legs and arms. Unable to reveal publicly the existence of a monster, yet unable to kill it, the family are said to have locked their offspring in a secret room built in the latter part of the seventeenth century. There it lived for years, its existence known only to the Earl of Strathmore, his heir and his factor.

Wild though this legend may be, it is long-lasting enough to suggest that there was, until fairly recently, a genuine secret concerning Glamis. The Earl of Strathmore was after his twenty-first birthday, according to Lord Halifax who knew him personally, 'a changed man. Silent, moody and never smiling.' In 1870, the resident Earl of Strathmore is quoted as saying to his wife: 'I have been to the secret chamber. I have learned what the secret is – and if you wish to please me, you will never mention the matter to me again.'

Over the years, guests have returned from Glamis with strange stories which only fuelled the gossip. Many said they were wakened in the night by animal-like howls and snarls, and one woman claimed she saw a pale face with huge, mournful eyes staring at her from a window across a courtyard. When it suddenly disappeared she heard appalling screams and watched as an old woman scurried across the yard carrying a large bundle.

In 1865, a workman who found a secret passage and claimed to have seen something alive in an adjoining room was given a large sum of money and induced to emigrate.

In 1870, a woman guest woke in her bedroom at Glamis to feel a beard brush against her face. As she fumbled for a light, the shape that had been standing next to her shambled into the next room where her son was sleeping. The boy's screams of terror brought the woman and her husband racing to his bedside. The boy began to explain that he had been wakened by a giant and, as he did so, all three were shaken by an almighty crash. At breakfast, the following morning, other guests said they too had heard the crash and one said she was wakened by the mournful whining of her dog. Their hosts, however, offered no explanation.

Dowager Lady Granville, the Queen Mother's sister, once said that as children they were never allowed to talk about the secret of Glamis. 'Our parents forbade us ever to discuss the matter or ask any questions about it,' she said. The present Queen's great-grandfather, the twelfth Earl, was quoted as saying: 'If you could only guess the nature of the secret, you would go down on your knees and thank God it was not yours!'

So just what is – or was – the secret of Glamis Castle? According to *Burke's Peerage*, Lord Glamis, heir to Thomas, eleventh Earl of Strathmore, married one Charlotte Grimstead in December 1820. They gave birth to a son and heir, Thomas George – later the twelfth Earl – who was born in September 1822. However, a closer look at the records suggests that Lord Glamis and his wife had another son, born in October 1821, who is said to have died shortly after his birth.

Today, experts suggest that this first-born son did not in fact die but was terribly deformed. He could never inherit the castle or the title and, although he was only expected to live for no more than a few days at most, he was well cared for. However, the child did live, surviving not only his father, but also his younger brother. It was a third son, Claude, who became the thirteenth Earl and he was succeeded in 1904 by his son – another Claude, born in 1855 – who was to become the father of the Queen Mother.

It is believed that the last heir to be initiated into the grim family secret was the fourteenth Earl, when he reached his twenty-first birthday in 1876. His son and successor, Timothy, was never told the secret although he once said: 'I feel sure there is a corpse or a coffin bricked up in the castle walls somewhere, but they are so thick one could search forever.'

Today, the legend of the monster of Glamis lives on in the name of a roof-top walkway, where the poor creature may have been exercised at night – the 'Mad Earl's Walk'. The Grey Lady still prays silently in the chapel. Ghosts still haunt the room where the Strathmores' personal executioner used to live and Earl Beardie is still seen, a huge old man with a flowing beard, sitting by the fire in one of the castle bedrooms.

The present Earl of Strathmore, Fergus Bowes-Lyon, dismisses all talk of ghosts and monsters as 'sheer guesswork and people's imagination running riot'. Perhaps it is, but the legend of the most terrible room in Britain lingers on!

Duntrune Castle stands about eighteen miles from Oban on the B8025 at Lochgilphead. It was built in the twelfth century and faces out over the waters of Loch Crinan. Set on a solid granite foundation on a small peak, surrounded by woodland, it is one of the most beautiful settings in the whole of Scotland. Once, Duntrune was a lonely fortress guarding the rich mainland from marauders, but in the sixteenth century a dwelling house was incorporated into its massive stone walls. Yet despite its age, Duntrune Castle appears to have little recorded history. One of the few details known about it is linked with the ghost which continues to haunt the ancient pile.

In the seventeenth century, an Irishman, Coll Ciotech, landed in Kintyre and marched north with his army, ravaging both people and property as he went. He was intent on destroying everything and everyone associated with his sworn enemies, the Campbells. On reaching Duntrune Castle he sent his piper in as a spy in an effort to establish the strength of its defences.

But the Campbells were not stupid. Although they admitted the piper, they were highly suspicious of him and locked him away in one of the castle turrets. Knowing he must warn his chief of the impregnable state of the castle and the strong army of well-armed Campbell supporters, the piper realized that the only way he could signal Coll Ciotech and warn him of the danger was with his pipes which, rather conveniently, the Campbells had forgotten to take from him.

Looking through his cell window high in the turret, he could see his Irish comrades approaching and he immediately began to play the pibroch – the piper's warning to his master. In the event he was successful, for Coll Ciotech turned about and returned to his ship. But by these actions the poor piper had signed his own death warrant. The Campbells, enraged at what he had done, cut off his fingers and then brutally slew him.

For many years the sound of his pipes haunted Duntrune Castle and early this century when some alterations were being carried out, a fingerless skeleton was discovered sealed in the ancient walls. At the time, the castle was tenanted by a clergyman and he gave the remains a Christian burial in order, so he thought, to put the spirit to rest. That was believed to be the end of the matter, but in the early 1970s it was revealed that the spirit was still active, with strange knockings on doors, pictures being flung from walls and heavy furniture and other objects being thrown about by invisible hands!

One reason for these continuing activities has been put forward as being due to the fact that the piper was possibly a member of the Irish Macdonnell clan, and therefore more than likely to have been a Roman Catholic. For him to have been buried in the enemy camp, by an Episcopal clergyman, in a church of the Protestant faith, was probably more than his fiery spirit could put up with!

Stirling Castle, some thirty-five miles to the north-west of Edinburgh, is said to be haunted by the prettiest ghost in Scotland in the form of a young woman dressed in a beautiful flowing gown of delicately woven shimmering pink silk.

No one seems to know just who she is, although there are those who believe this could well be the shade of Mary, Queen of Scots, who was crowned in the castle chapel when she was less than twelve months old. It is suggested that her pretty ghost returns to one of the few places where she found happiness in her short, tragic life.

However, the most likely explanation as to the identity of this pretty spectre goes back to the reign of Edward I of England, when the castle was under siege by his troops in 1303. The story goes that one brave young woman insisted on staying by her husband's side, but she was persuaded for her own safety to leave. She was smuggled out just before the surviving 150 or so defenders surrendered and has been searching in vain for her husband ever since.

I am told that the best vantage point for anyone wishing to see this ghost is from what is known as 'Ladies' Rock'. This stands in a sort of gulley between the castle and the church in the old tilting ground and it was from this rock that the womenfolk of old would sit to watch the jousting.

Nearly every American knows of Culzean Castle, and every year thousands of them visit the place, simply because one apartment in the castle was presented to General Eisenhower back in 1946.

The castle, built in the eighteenth century for the Earls of Cassilis, stands on the A719 about ten miles south-west of Ayr. The family burial place is at nearby Maybole Church, itself on the site of an ancient church founded by Duncan, Earl of Carrick, in about 1160.

Close by stand the ruins of the Collegiate church and it is from here that the ghost of the famous Kennedy piper sets out to pipe his mournful music in Culzean Castle. The ghostly music is usually heard on stormy nights, carried on the wind. On a number of occasions over the years, the piper's spectre has been seen drifting among the large rhododendron bushes which surround the castle. According to tradition, the ghostly piper is said to play to herald the marriage of a future head of the Kennedy family, former owners of the castle.

There is a rather interesting legend surrounding Culzean Castle which tells of how one laird met a small boy carrying a wooden bucket who begged him for some ale for his sick mother. The laird sent him to his butler with orders to have the bucket filled. But after a half-filled barrel was emptied and the small bucket remained unfilled, the mystified butler was loath to broach a new barrel. However, he obeyed the laird's orders and, to his amazement, scarcely a drop had flowed from the new barrel than the little bucket was overflowing. Without a word of thanks, the boy took it to his mother.

Many years later, the same laird was taken prisoner in the wars in Flanders. He was suspected of being a spy and was sentenced to be hanged. On the night before his execution, his cell door suddenly flew open and the same small boy magically appeared. Taking the laird on his shoulders, he carried him with the speed of light back to Culzean Castle. As the ghostly boy left the laird he turned and said: 'One guid turn deserves anither. Tak ye that for bein' sae kind to ma auld mither.'

Another legend tells us that one laird of Culzean had a daughter called May who was carried off by an evil knight called Sir John, to Games Loup Rock on the Ayrshire coast. Here, he told the girl that he had already drowned seven wives and she was to be next. He ordered her to strip naked and, modestly, she begged him to turn his back. Sir John obeyed, but as soon as he did so May rushed at him and pushed him off the rock and into the sea, where he drowned.

Although the local version of the legend names the murderous knight as 'false Sir John', in an older ballad he is the supernatural elf-knight, who abducts the heiress of Culzean and tells her he is going to kill her. But she lulls him to sleep with a charm, steals his dirk and stabs him to death!

The sixteenth-century Pencait Castle stands about twenty miles to the east of Edinburgh between Fordel Mains and Haddington, on the A6093.

According to local tradition there are said to be at least three ghosts here, although perhaps the best known is that which is associated with a four-poster bed once belonging to King Charles I. In the 1920s, Pencait Castle was owned by Sir Andrew Lauder who was given the bed in which the King had slept, as a gift. Not long after it had been installed, Sir Andrew invited a friend to have a look at his magnificent acquisition. Both men were surprised, however, to discover that the bedding was crumpled, as if the bed had recently been slept in, despite the fact that the door to the room had been locked for some time.

About sixty years ago, a young woman staying at Pencait was occupying this same bed in what had now become known as the 'King Charles Room'. She was disturbed in the small hours by what sounded like burglars moving about downstairs and she woke the occupants. A thorough search was made but no one could be found. Nothing appeared to have been disturbed and the doors and windows were still securely fastened.

Mystified, but satisfied that all was as it should be, the occupants, servants and young woman decided to return to their comfortable beds. As they returned upstairs, however, they all suddenly heard an unmistakable creaking noise coming from the King Charles Room. It sounded just as if someone having a disturbed night was turning over in bed – the very four-poster bed vacated just minutes before by the young woman!

An interesting legend surrounding Pencait Castle concerns a local beggar, Alexander Hamilton. According to the story, Hamilton called at the castle one day many years ago, and received a none-too-pleasant welcome from the owner's wife, who told him in no uncertain terms to clear off and slammed the door in his face. Hamilton, who was reputed to dabble in sorcery, returned to the castle in the dead of night and bound the bars of the castle gates with 'murderous intent'.

A few days later, the lady of the house and her eldest daughter were struck down by a mysterious fatal illness. Alexander Hamilton, who apparently had been bragging throughout the area that he had bewitched the household, was quickly arrested and brought to trial on a charge of witchcraft. He seemed only too happy to confess to being responsible not only for the deaths of the two women by witchery, but also to a variety of unresolved crimes in the area. Found guilty, he was hanged at the Edinburgh Grassmarket.

We are told that ever since that time, on certain nights of the year, Hamilton's ghost returns to Pencait Castle, his evil spirit still seeking to avenge itself!

Cawdor Castle stands on the B9090 ten miles to the north-east of Inverness, and within five miles of the battlefield of Culloden.

According to legend, when William Cawdor chose his site for his castle, he loaded his donkey with gold and let the animal roam the moors for a day until it lay down exhausted at the foot of a hawthorn bush. On this exact spot Cawdor built his castle in about 1370, and the hawthorn can still be found today, growing in the centre.

Scientists recently determined the precise age of the hawthorn tree and have confirmed that it does go back to the fourteenth century – a fact which continues to amaze many visitors.

Something else which often amazes visitors is the almost

nightly appearance of the slim ghost of an attractive young woman with no hands, who walks among the ruins surrounding the castle. During Cawdor's often turbulent history, the castle was besieged on a number of occasions. Several hundred years ago, when the ancestors of the present owners were attacked by a rival clan, their pretty young daughter fell madly in love with the son of the enemy chieftain. She appears to have been so smitten that she could hardly keep the romance a secret and, according to legend, confided in a member of the household who immediately informed the girl's father.

The Earl of Cawdor was so enraged at his daughter's disloyalty that he pursued the terrified girl to the topmost turret of the castle. Unable to escape, she climbed out of a window and hung from the turret clasping the bars. Her merciless father hacked off her hands with his sword and she fell from the tower to her death, which is why, to this day, the unfortunate girl continues to haunt the castle lingering at the base of the ill-fated tower near the ancient hawthorn tree.

Braemar Castle lies a few miles south-west of Balmoral, on the A93, and has been haunted by a mysterious blonde woman for over a century.

The castle, now belonging to Captain Farquharson of Invercauld, was built around 1628. The ghostly blonde temptress appears every time the Farquharsons invite a honeymoon couple to stay. I am told that her last appearance was in 1987 when one young bridegroom had just finished writing a letter in the panelled library and on returning to his bedroom, saw his wife leaving the room by the opposite door. He called out to her but she took no notice, which surprised him – and he was even more surprised when, some minutes later, he found her in another part of the castle. She swore she had not been in the bedroom!

When Captain Farquharson was told of the incident, he related the story of a strange incident which had taken place at Braemar over a century ago and which accounted for the unusual experience.

It appears that last century another incident occurred when his ancestors were entertaining a newly-wed couple. The day after the wedding night, the husband left at dawn to go hunting, and his young wife, thinking he had deserted her, was so grief-stricken by his sudden disappearance that she committed suicide and was subsequently buried at Braemar. From time to time, she returns to the guest's bedroom in search of a young bridegroom – any young bridegroom – who might be sleeping there!

The cobwebs are still intact and even the dust is said to be original at Traquair Castle, about seven miles from Galashiels, which is the haunt of a very demanding ghost according to the late Peter Maxwell-Stuart. He had sworn never to alter the 'spooky room' in the cellar which is haunted by his favourite ancestor, Bonnie Prince Charlie.

Traquair dates back to 1107 and has reputedly been visited by no less than sixty kings and queens. Peter Maxwell-Stuart was in fact a direct descendant of Mary, Queen of Scots, and the most regular apparition is that of his other illustrious ancestor, Charles Edward Stuart, who left Traquair to fight the English. As he passed through the Bear Gates of Traquair Castle, Bonnie Prince Charlie ordered that the huge monumental gate, representing two stone bears, should be left closed until he returned victor over the English.

But Charles Edward Stuart, a fervent Catholic, never returned to Traquair Castle; he died a querulous drunk in Rome in 1789, since when the gates have never been opened. Now, on certain evenings when the wind howls over the Scottish countryside, one can hear, and often see, the solitary ghost of Bonnie Prince Charlie walking up the abandoned path leading to the Bear Gates.

Fyvie Castle, just off the A947 between Turriff and Old Meldrum, stands some twenty-seven miles to the north-west of Aberdeen. The castle is famous, not only for its ghost, but also for its secret chamber.

The castle's famous Grey Lady was frequently seen during the 1920s and 1930s, when she was at her most active, wandering forlornly along the corridors and disappearing through the oak panels of one of the rooms. At some time in the early 1920s, a large fungus had appeared on one of the walls in the gun room and when workmen removed it, and were treating the woodwork, they discovered a secret panel behind which was a skeleton.

This discovery sparked off a series of paranormal disturbances until Lord Leith, who then owned the castle, gave
instructions for the skeleton to be replaced behind the panelling
of the wall. Normality of a sort returned, but ever since, the Grey
Lady has shown herself to several startled visitors over the
years. Like many other Scottish castles, Fyvie has a phantom
drummer.

Jedburgh Castle stands just sixteen miles inside the Scottish
border at the junction of the A68 and B6356. Built on the
foundations of an original twelfth-century structure, the present
façade is nineteenth-century. Here, on certain occasions, a tall
dark figure, hooded and cloaked, manifests itself. This is no
modern ghost, for this harbinger of death has appeared to many
people for well over 700 years.

One of the best-documented incidents is said to have taken
place as far back as 1285, when in October of that year King
Alexander III of Scotland married Yolande, the pretty daughter
of the Count of Druix. Alexander was in his mid-forties and had
taken a new bride in the hope that she would bear him a male
heir and thus secure the Scottish throne. So the wedding feast
was a joyous occasion with plenty of food, freely flowing ale and
entertainment provided by mummers and tumblers for the
many assembled guests.

Suddenly, a tall cowled figure appeared in the corner of the
Great Hall, the noise and music fading into an abrupt nervous
silence. Such was the power of the mysterious stranger that
everyone present felt some apprehension, for the figure wore a
death mask and his clothing hinted of some grave sacred rite.
Who or what dared to threaten the happiness of the King?

As most of the revellers gaped in terror, the silent figure
glided through the crowd, none of whom dared to lay a hand on
him. Then, one huge Highland chieftain, braver than the rest,
lunged at the cloaked figure with the intention of throwing him
from the battlements for daring to play such a tasteless joke on
his King's wedding day. But the figure simply disintegrated in
his hands and the startled Highlander was left clutching the
empty cloak and mask. There was little doubt in the minds of all
those present that ill-luck and possible death was about to fall
on their King.

Their fears were justified, for six months later King Alexander was riding back to Edinburgh following a visit to Kinghorn. It was a wild and stormy night and his horse suddenly stumbled, throwing the King over Ha'craig Point where he subsequently drowned in the Firth of Forth. The thing which Alexander most feared had happened. He had died without a male heir and so Scotland would be plunged into yet another bloody struggle for the crown.

The Castle of Mey – sometimes called Barrowgill Castle – is the Caithness home of the Queen Mother and stands just off the A836, midway between Dunnet and John o'Groats.

Here one will find another Green Lady who died for love. According to tradition, the daughter of the fifth Earl of Caithness fell in love with a ploughman and was imprisoned by her irate father in the uppermost room of the tower. So that she could not see her lover at work, one of the tower windows was bricked up. Broken-hearted, the young woman is said to have jumped to her death from the other window. As the Green Lady, her mournful wraith is still seen drifting through the castle to this day.

Meggernie Castle stands roughly halfway up Glen Lyon in Perth, almost in the physical heart of Scotland. The oldest parts of the castle date back to the fifteenth century and are characterized by walls several feet thick. Originally it was the property of the Clan McGregor, but was taken from them in the late sixteenth century as punishment for their opposition to the throne. Since then it has passed through various hands and during the latter half of the last century was owned by Mr Herbert Wood, a hospitable man who enjoyed nothing better than having his castle full of guests.

One such guest at this time was Leicester businessman, Mr E.J. Simons. It was late at night and the other guests and their hosts had already gone to bed. However, Mr Simons wished to catch the next day's post and had gone into the library to write some letters.

As he bent over the writing table he became aware that the atmosphere in the room had become so cold he was beginning to shiver. Yet, when he glanced towards the huge fireplace, the large logs were blazing on a deep bed of glowing embers. Suddenly a feeling of unaccountable fear enveloped him.

Glancing round the room to see if anyone was there, he saw no one, but his attention was drawn to the heavy studded door which led to the corridor outside. It was slowly and noiselessly opening. As he stared at the door, unable to take his eyes off it, he saw the upper half of a woman's body glide by and pass down the corridor outside. With a tremendous effort of will, he put down his pen, picked up the lamp by which he had been writing, and frozen with fear, he forced himself to set off for his bedroom with the intention of taking refuge there.

However, to get to his bedroom, he had first to pass down a long flagged passage on the ground floor. The passage contained only a single window and, as he passed it, he saw the face of a beautiful woman, which bore an expression of infinite sadness, peering through the glass. This brought him to a sudden halt. But even in the beam of his lamp, which shone fully on it, the tragic face appeared to be undisturbed. It remained looking in through the window long enough for him to obtain a good look at the features. Then suddenly it was gone!

Round about the turn of the century, one of the young housemaids ran screaming hysterically to her mistress that she had seen a ghost. When she had calmed down, she said that the *lower* part of the woman – from the waist downwards – had passed her and moved quickly along one of the corridors leading to the north tower. The lower part of the gown, which covered the legs, was splattered with blood where the waist should have been.

In 1928, a local doctor was called to the castle late one night. As it was so late and he lived some distance away, he gratefully accepted an invitation to stay for the night. He was put in a room in the tower and was soon asleep. But he woke up after about an hour thinking he had heard footsteps approaching his door. He suspected that he was going to be summoned to his patient, but as he waited for the knock on his door – which never came – he had the distinct impression that someone had entered the room.

As he glanced round the dark bedroom he saw, illuminated in a sort of pink light, a woman's head and shoulders gliding round the walls of the room high up near the ceiling. As he watched it, the figure suddenly evaporated.

Over the years other members of the household have seen this apparition and there are several former servants and people who live in Glen Lyon who testify to having seen the ghostly legs, not only wandering the castle, but also in the avenue of limes and in the graveyard. Even within the past decade, occupants of the castle have heard inexplicable rappings and knockings.

The explanation behind this 'ghost in two halves' appears to go back to the days when Meggernie Castle formed part of the estate of the Clan Menzies. The chief had a very beautiful wife who was constantly attracting the attention of the local gentry and Menzies, an extremely jealous man, attacked her in one of his frenzied rages. He hit her and she fell catching her head on the bedpost and dying within a few minutes.

To hide his crime, Menzies sawed her body in two halves. One half he deposited in a makeshift grave in the churchyard and the other he buried under the floor between the joists of one of the bedrooms in the tower. This, according to tradition, is why the upper half of the Meggernie ghost haunts the rooms of the tower while the lower half wanders about the ground floor corridors and the avenue of limes.

Cullen House, near Aberdeen, is a huge fortress-like pile of granite blocks, heraldic beasts, gargoyles, coats of arms, all crowned by a jumble of towers, turrets, mossy slates and little windows rearing up against a background of grey sky.

Soon after the defeat of Bonnie Prince Charlie in 1746, Cullen was inherited by James, sixth Earl of Findlater and third Earl of Seafield. He was known as the 'Mad Earl', for he was permanently insane and would periodically be seized by some form of fit, during which time he would become violent. He may have suffered from some extreme form of epilepsy, because he always knew when a seizure was coming on and would lock himself in the library and drop the key out of the window. Then, when he had sufficiently recovered, his factor, who was his closest friend, would let him out.

On 3 November 1770, James had one of his fits, but his factor returned too soon and when the Earl came round he was to discover that he had murdered his friend. Horror-stricken, the Mad Earl rushed from the room, stumbled up the spiral staircase to the tower and went into the attics. There he committed suicide by cutting his throat. Since that time, the ghost of the Mad Earl has walked the corridors and staircase of Cullen.

In 1943, a housemaid nearly witnessed a re-enaction of the tragedy when one afternoon, with the family away, she went into the library to dust. To her astonishment she saw an elderly man sitting in one of the big armchairs. She said later that she got the impression the figure was that of a kindly person. He was smiling and watching someone who was seated at the desk, but she was too nervous to look and see who the other person was, though she could see his figure from the corner of her eye. The atmosphere of the room seemed very strained because although the old gentleman seated in the armchair was smiling, he looked ill at ease and possibly frightened.

Thinking that the two men were staying at the house, the little maid apologized and left the room. In a bedroom a few yards away she met the head housemaid who told her that there was no one staying at the house. The maid insisted that she came and saw for herself, but when they re-entered the library the room was empty. What she had seen was the ghost of the murdered factor, and the shadowy figure at the desk would have been the shade of the Mad Earl himself.

In 1964, two hard-bitten Fleet Street reporters were invited to stay at Cullen, more as a challenge than to investigate the ghost. Like most newsmen they were highly sceptical of the paranormal, but after three nights they came away convinced the old place was well and truly haunted.

On arrival, one was given the 'Pulpit Room' at the head of the spiral staircase. The other was given the 'Church Room' just around the corner; a large room with two modern twin beds, enormous windows and a luxurious thick pile carpet. Opposite was a modern bathroom and the passage outside was short, thickly carpeted, and stopped at a low door in the wall which led to the attics. There was nothing spooky about the rooms and nothing to stimulate the imagination.

Tired after their long journey from London, the journalists went to bed early, expecting to go to sleep almost at once, but one of them later reported: 'I began to realize that the atmosphere of my room was changing. Very slowly, so slowly as to be almost imperceptible. I felt a growing thickness, an increasing oppression as if a thunderstorm was gathering in the room. As it grew stronger I felt the symptoms of fever; my body was alternating between heat and icy shivers; I had difficulty in breathing evenly; my heart pounded and I felt a vague, illogical distress.'

The man lay for about an hour and a half before he suddenly heard footsteps. At first the sounds seemed far away and he thought his imagination was beginning to play tricks on him. But then he knew it was no trick of the mind; they were footsteps and they were coming up the stairs towards his bedroom. The footsteps sounded uneven, appearing to stumble every now and then. They were not in the least furtive as he could distinctly hear the scrape of leather on stone. He said: 'I felt no fear – until I suddenly remembered something which made my flesh crawl. I could hear feet on stone – but the stairs were thickly carpeted!'

The footsteps stumbled round the corner of the passage and stopped outside the newspaperman's door. He sat up and stared at the door handle, terrified that it might turn. A cold sweat trickled down his chest. For a second or two the door handle seemed to tremble, then the footsteps retreated, slowly dying away.

Other people have had similar experiences in this room. One man reported hearing a frightful noise coming from there, when he and his wife slept in the bedroom directly beneath. They knew that the room was supposed to be empty. The sound of footsteps on the stairs and someone tramping about is an all-too-common occurrence. One person was so disturbed while sleeping in the Church Room that he rushed downstairs at three o'clock in the morning and refused to sleep there ever again!

The Mad Earl, it seems, is somehow tied to Cullen House, returning periodically with the same agitation and agony of mind that he had when he was alive.

At the end of the seventeenth century, trouble flared up between the Covenanters – the militant Presbyterians – and Royalists of the Episcopalian faith.

The most famous of the Royalist generals at that time was John Graham, Viscount Dundee, of Cloverhouse. Known to his friends as Bonnie Dundee, his enemies believed him to be a warlock. In 1689, he raised the clans to fight for James II against William III who was supported by the Covenanters, and many of the ruling gentry of southern Scotland rode to join him.

Lord Balcarres of Colinsburgh Castle – which stands just off the A921 about three miles east of Largo, in Fife – was prevented from joining him because he had been placed under house arrest by Parliament. While Lord Balcarres fretted in inactivity, his friend Dundee fought his last and greatest battle at Killiecrankie, and according to tradition was killed by a silver bullet at the moment of victory. At dawn the following morning, Lord Balcarres awoke to find his friend gazing sorrowfully at him from his bedside. Not knowing he was dead, Balcarres got up to greet him – and Dundee disappeared!

Apparently, the ghost of Dundee was seen on several occasions during Lord Balcarres life, but so far as I am aware it has not been seen since. It is interesting to note why Dundee was alleged to have been killed by a silver bullet. His enemies believed him to be a warlock and they also believed this was the only means of killing off supernatural creatures.

The sixteenth-century Noltland Castle at Westray on the island of Orkney was once the home of the Balfours, and the ruins are haunted by a number of family phantoms, including a monster called Broonie who is said to have built roads and pulled boats to safety during storms. But the best-known phenomenon at Noltland Castle was the spectral light which illuminated whenever a member of the Balfour family was born or married. Deaths were said to have been announced by the howling of another of the castle's phantoms, the 'Boky Hound'.

Gight Castle, three miles north of Methlick on the B9005, north-west of Aberdeen, has for many years been haunted by a ghostly piper. According to legend, a piper was once sent to explore an underground passage leading from the castle; his progress followed from above by the sound of his pipes. Although his pipes were, and still are, occasionally, heard quite clearly, the piper was never seen again.

The fourteenth century Ruthven Castle at Kingussie on the A9, about twelve miles south-west of Aviemore, was once the home of King Robert II's son, Alexander, a man whose ruthlessness rapidly earned him the title of 'Wolf of Badenoch'. Despite the scandalized protests of the Church, he refused to abandon his mistress and return to his wife. As a punishment, he was excommunicated and he sought his revenge by burning Elgin Cathedral to the ground.

Alexander and his marauders became the terror of the district, pillaging by day and dabbling in witchcraft by night. Then, one stormy evening, watching villagers saw a sinister figure dressed in black ride up to Ruthven Castle. Creeping nearer, some of the bolder villagers peered through a window and saw the stranger engrossed in a game of chess with the Wolf of Badenoch. The stranger moved a chess-piece and laughed. 'Check,' he cried, and at once the scene was blotted out by a wall of fire.

The villagers fled in terror, but when they returned the next morning they found the bodies of Alexander and his followers among the blackened ruins of the castle. Even to this day, it is said that on occasions the ghosts of Alexander and his men can still be seen there, endlessly playing a phantom game of chess!

The ruins of Buckholme Tower, near Galashiels, are all that is left of a once grim fortress and are reputedly haunted by the ghost of Laird Pringle: a sadistic man who treated his own family so badly that they left him to his own devices and were never heard of again. All this took place over two hundred years ago, since when, strange noises have been heard coming from the ancient Tower dungeon and blood has repeatedly oozed from an old oak beam.

After his family left him, Laird Pringle's behaviour became insanely violent and one of his greatest pleasures in life, apart from drink, was to hound the militant Presbyterians, or Covenanters, whose form of worship had been outlawed by the English Parliament.

One day, the Laird was called on to assist a troop of Redcoats in breaking up an unlawful assembly of Covenanters who were known to be gathering near Glendearg. More than eager to help, he arrived at the meeting place only to find the Covenanters had been forwarned and had disbanded. All had gone, except for an old man and his son, both of whom were well-known Covenanters.

Laird Pringle was all for killing them there and then but he was prevented from doing so by the Redcoat officer, who suggested that it might be better if they were taken back to Buckholme Tower. They could then be placed in the dungeon until the next day, to await torture by the soldiers in an effort to extract information from them regarding their fellow worshippers. Pringle agreed and the unfortunate pair were returned to the Tower and thrown into the grim dungeon, a place which can still be seen today, with its row of iron hooks suspended high in the ceiling.

However, Pringle couldn't wait for the return of the soldiers and late that night servants were wakened by horrific cries of agony coming from the dungeon. A few of the bolder servants went to investigate and as they neared the dungeon door the Laird stumbled out saying that swine should be treated as swine. He staggered towards the main door and, when he opened it, there was an old woman standing there. It was the old man's wife looking for her menfolk. Grabbing hold of her, Pringle dragged her inside and across to the dungeon, where a piercing scream broke from her lips when she saw, suspended from the hooks in the ceiling, like the carcasses of pigs, the bleeding bodies of her husband and son. Wild-eyed and screaming, the old woman ran out of the dungeon only to fall headlong to the ground where, for some time she lay sobbing hysterically. With a cruel smile on his lips, Pringle stood over her.

But the smile was to turn to a look of fear when, slowly and deliberately, the old woman struggled to her feet and, controlling herself with a great deal of effort, quietly and calmly called the wrath of God down on his head, saying that his deeds, like the hounds of Hell, should haunt him day and night for the rest of his wicked life. He would find no rest either in this world or the next.

For the remainder of his life, Laird Pringle believed himself to be haunted. He would wake up in the night screaming with terror as he imagined some ghostly hound tearing at his throat. It was not long after that he died, following a long and painful illness, full of terror at the last moments, his body shaking with convulsions as if it was being torn apart by savage hounds.

Locals will tell you that today, usually around the anniversary of his death, a ghostly figure can be seen in the vicinity of Buckholme Tower: a figure which appears to be running for its life from a pack of baying hounds. The sound of dogs is often heard coming from the dungeon itself, sometimes accompanied by terrified cries, frenzied breathing and blood-curdling screams which are then followed by an ominous silence!

Finally, Cortachy Castle, just off the B955 north of Kirriemuir, is said to be haunted by a phantom drummer. Through the treachery of a Cameron drummer who deliberately failed to give warning of the enemy's advance, Lord Ogilvy's house – the

Bonnie Hoose o' Airlie – was burnt to the ground during the seventeenth-century wars of the Covenant.

The angry defenders picked up the drummer and threw him and his drum into the flames and as a result, it is said that even today, when an Ogilvy is about to die at Cortachy Castle, his phantom drumbeat can be heard throughout the castle and its grounds.

# 2　Ghosts With
# and Without Reason

There is good evidence for 'ghosts with a purpose'; apparitions which seem to materialize for some specific reason and which are seen no more once the matter is resolved. Far more difficult to define is the ghost which appears without any obvious reason and is only seen once, or by a small handful of people over a short period of time, before it suddenly ceases to haunt just as mysteriously as it began.

The following is a typical example which took place in the Celtic Craft Centre in Edinburgh in 1984, and which was related to me by Mrs Alison Berg of Kelso.

She told me: 'If you had told me five years ago that such things could happen, or that there really were ghosts, I would have laughed at you. But since my experience at the Celtic Craft Centre, which has never been resolved, I have an altogether different outlook on the whole subject of the supernatural.'

It was during the quiet season, when Edinburgh steps back to catch its breath between the tourist season and the Festival. Mrs Berg was alone in the shop when she heard someone knocking in the basement. Knowing that the man who usually worked there, parcelling up and posting souvenirs and gifts to various parts of the world, was not working on that particular day, she automatically assumed it was her boss playing some kind of trick on her. Closing the shop door, Mrs Berg went down the stairs to see what he was doing and was surprised to discover the basement was empty.

She said: 'As the basement was empty I thought that perhaps the knocking must have been coming from one of the other shops, so I dismissed it from my mind and returned upstairs. As I came back into the shop, I looked through the tie rack and saw

34

a man standing at the counter. He was as solid-looking and as three-dimensional as you are, and I could see he was dressed in tweeds. I automatically thought I had a customer, but by the time I had taken two steps he was gone. Yet the shop door had not opened and there was no other way he could have got out.'

Apparently this is not the only strange incident to have taken place here. Mrs Berg tells me that the owner of the Craft Centre has a photograph of the interior of the building, taken when it was empty, which quite distinctly shows a person sitting above the level of the present shop floor. So far as I am aware, there have been no other incidents at the shop.

On the other side of the coin, a row in the House of Commons during the First World War may have been responsible for the mysterious reappearance of a long-dead pilot, who returned to haunt his former airbase three years after the crash that killed him.

Pemberton Billing MP, head of the Southampton firm which was later to develop the Spitfire, accused the government in 1916 of doing nothing while certain Royal Flying Corps men were 'murdered rather than killed by the carelessness, incompetence or ignorance of their senior officers or of the technical side of the service'.

One of the cases he cited was that of Desmond Arthur, an Irish Lieutenant with No. 2 Squadron RFC, who died in a crash over the airbase at Montrose in May 1913. Arthur was gliding down from four thousand feet, preparing to land, when the starboard wing of his BE2 biplane folded in mid-air. As the tiny aircraft plunged to the ground, the pilot's seatbelt snapped and he was thrown out of the cockpit. There were no parachutes in 1913, so ground staff could only watch helplessly as he fell to his death, arms and legs flailing.

The Royal Aero Club's accidents investigation committee began an immediate inquiry, and concluded that an unautho-rised repair job on the plane's right wing had been botched and then covered up. Someone had broken a wing spar near the tip, repaired it with a crude splice, then concealed the work by stretching new fabric over the affected area. To Lieutenant Arthur's friends in the RFC, it added up to murder, but the offender could not be pinpointed.

Billing used the Aero Club's findings as a basis for his 1916 onslaught in Parliament. He was as astonished as anyone when the government, anxious as always to avoid scandal that might undermine public faith in its war effort, issued its own report on the crash. It said the wing repair explanation was based on the evidence of only one of twenty-three witnesses, and was completely without any foundation whatever. In other words, Arthur had only himself to blame for the crash! An interim report was issued on 3 August 1916 and a detailed version was promised before Christmas.

In September, a month after the publication of the interim report, airmen based at Montrose began to notice a number of curious things. Twice, one officer followed a tall figure in full flying kit towards the mess, only to see him vanish before reaching the door. One night, a flying instructor woke up to find a strange man sitting in a chair beside the fire in his bedroom. When he sat up and challenged the intruder, he was astounded to see the figure suddenly vanish into thin air. Two other airmen woke simultaneously one night, convinced a third person was in their room and yet, when they turned the lamp up, the room was empty!

Was Lieutenant Desmond Arthur trying to rally his friends in the Royal Flying Corps to clear his name? It would appear so. As the story of the hauntings began to spread around other airbases, two of the government's committee of inquiry revealed that they had not even seen the Royal Aero Club's findings which their interim report had denigrated!

After studying the results of the earlier investigation, Sir Charles Bright, an engineer, and a lawyer called Butcher, added an amendment to the final report when it was issued that Christmas. They declared: 'It appears probable that the machine had been damaged accidentally, and that the man (or men) responsible for the damage had repaired it as best he (or they) could to evade detection and punishment.'

The ghost of Lieutenant Arthur appears to have settled for this as an indication of his innocence in causing the crash, for after one last appearance in January 1917, the phantom flyer has never been seen again.

Near Leverburgh on the southern tip of Harris, there once lived a very old woman who had been bedridden for a number of years.

One day, as she lay dying in a four-poster bed in an upstairs room of the isolated cottage where she lived alone, she confided to her doctor that she had hidden all her wealth – a bag full of gold coins – under her mattress. The doctor, an avaricious man without any scruples whatsoever, pretended to attend to her, and while doing so, slipped his hand under the mattress and stole the bag. But as he did so the old woman roused herself and, with her dying breath, cursed the doctor saying that his clutching hand would never find peace in the grave. It would remain earthbound 'till the Day of Judgement'.

According to legend, the doctor was the only person present when the old lady died and when she had breathed her last he drew the curtains round her. Friends ordered the local joiner to make a coffin and send it to the house. It was duly delivered and was to be received by the doctor. When the mourners arrived on the day of the funeral, they were surprised to discover the coffin had already been sealed and the lid well screwed down.

Four villagers, acting as bearers, picked up the coffin to carry it to the local churchyard, and they were heard to remark that the old woman must have wasted away to nothing, as the coffin was so light. It was interred with due reverence and the mourners returned to the cottage for the traditional refreshment. There they were horrified to discover that the old woman's corpse was still behind the curtains in the four-poster bed. Unbeknown to them the doctor, not daring to risk being seen leaving the cottage with a bag of gold had, with the help of the joiner, smuggled it out in the coffin, to be retrieved later. The doctor and the gold disappeared and neither was seen again.

For years the story was treated as pure legend and various crofters and their families lived in the cottage over the next hundred years or more, without ever experiencing anything untoward. But all this was to change earlier this century when a young woman, touring the Outer Hebrides, lost her way in the evening mist and sought sanctuary at the remote cottage.

After supper with the crofter and his wife, she was shown to her room, which was small, low-ceilinged and appeared to have been unused for years. Something about it made her feel uneasy, and this was not helped by the piteous howling of a dog outside, mingled with the shriek of a night wind coming in from the Atlantic. The young woman closed the window and bolted the bedroom door, but, even then, for some reason, she did not feel safe. The candle cast eerie shadows on the ceiling and there was a musty odour in the room, which she put down to the fact that it was barely used. However, the bed looked inviting so she quickly undressed, climbed in exhausted, and very soon fell asleep.

In the small hours she was suddenly wakened by the loud moaning of the wind. There was a crash at the window, followed by the sound of breaking glass. The curtains billowed into the room seeming to draw something in with them – what, she couldn't tell. There was an overpowering smell of putrifying meat which was so strong it made her feel sick, and there was more whining coming from the dog outside.

Then, in the darkness, a cold clammy hand gripped her ankle with fingers of steel. The young woman was too terrified to move, especially when the hand moved up to her throat. She had the horrifying thought that someone was about to strangle her and she seized hold of the hand, only to discover it was attached to a strong sinewy arm. But the arm ended in space as there was no body attached to it! Needless to say, the young woman fainted in terror.

When she awoke it was morning. There was no wind and the room was flooded with strong sunlight. She dismissed the previous night's experience as a nightmare, that is until she saw the broken window-pane which was evidence that someone or something had entered her room during the night. When she got out of bed she caught sight of herself in the mirror. Angry bruising around her throat proved that the horrifying experience had not been a dream.

In 1838, Father Charles McKay, a Roman Catholic priest with a parish in Perth, was visited by a woman called Anne Simpson. She told him that she was 'terribly troubled at night' by a ghostly woman who kept appearing to her. Mrs Simpson told the priest that she was a Presbyterian, and when he asked her why she had come to him rather than to her own minister, she replied: 'But sir, the woman asked me to go to the priest'. She said the figure had told her that she owed three shillings and ninepence and the priest would pay it.

Mrs Simpson protested that she was not trying to obtain money for herself, nor had she been dreaming, for the ghostly apparition appeared every single night, allowing her no rest.

She said she recognized the figure as that of a woman called Mrs Molloy, who she often saw during her lifetime going in and out of the military barracks at Perth.

Following these disclosures, Father McKay made several enquiries and was surprised to discover that there had been a woman who worked as a washerwoman at the barracks, and she had been called Mrs Molloy. She had indeed died fairly recently and what is more, she had owed the sum of three shillings and ninepence to a grocer in the town.

Father McKay paid the debt and later he called to see Anne Simpson, who told him that she was no longer troubled by the apparition. This was a classic example of a ghost coming with a mission of bidding to the living.

I was told of a certain Edinburgh hospital which possesses a haunted ward. Some years ago a young man met with an accident in an Edinburgh street and was taken to the hospital where he was put in a cubicle on Ward D.

On the third night he was lying in bed half awake when two nurses came into the cubicle with a trolley and proceeded to give him an injection. Then they lifted him out of bed and laid him on the trolley, which they then pushed out of the ward and into a room where two doctors, in white coats and with surgical masks over their faces, waited for him. One of them bent over, and the patient noticed that he had a dark beard and dark gleaming eyes full of fiendish hatred. In fact, the doctor seemed intent on killing him.

The young patient began to scream and the nurses who had attended to him tried to calm him down, and then their voices weakened and faded away altogether. When his brain cleared and he recognized his surroundings, he was back in his cubicle on Ward D.

Some time after he had been discharged, he was to recall his experience with one of the hospital staff. 'Were you on Ward D?' was the response. Then he was told that this particular ward had a reputation for being haunted. Apparently, not all that many years ago, there had been two doctors there, Dr McKay and Dr McGowan, an anaesthetist. Both men loved the same pretty young blonde and, although they had once been great friends, their rivalry for the affections of the girl had since made them deadly enemies. Dr McKay was knocked down by a car in

Comiston Road and seriously injured. He was taken to the hospital where he was placed on Ward D. There it was discovered that an emergency operation was necessary. The surgeon who was called to do the operation was Mr Warren and the anaesthetist was none other than McKay's rival, Dr McGowan. McGowan administered the anaesthetic, deliberately overdoing it and murdering McKay in what he considered to be the perfect crime. Later he married the young girl and shortly afterwards left the hospital.

But McGowan himself met with a fatal accident and just before he died he confessed to his crime. It was after this that Ward D, which McKay had occupied, began to be haunted.

There are several people living both in southern Scotland, and in northern Cumbria, who claim to have witnessed the spectacle of a phantom ship sailing along the Solway Firth. One old gentleman I spoke to claimed to have seen it on a number of occasions, usually around Christmas time.

It was Christmas Eve as the slave ship *Betsy Jane* sailed down the coast of the Solway. All along the coast, church bells could be heard ringing out the joy of Christmas, but the skipper of the *Betsy Jane* could think only of the gold that would line his pocket the following Christmas. Once out of the Firth, he steered the *Betsy Jane* on a southerly course heading for the coast of Africa to trade in the profitable cargo of human beings. Load after load of slaves he had carried under terrible conditions, shipping them to western countries, as his purse grew fatter. The more bodies he could ship and sell, the more gold for his greedy palm. For he had but one great ambition left in life – to finish his career at sea by sailing back up the Solway a wealthy man.

At last his greed was satisfied and, when the sun was low, he sailed the *Betsy Jane* for Scotland and home, timing his return to reach the Solway Firth on Christmas morning, as he had always boasted he would do. As the days passed on the homeward voyage, he gloated over the heavy load of glittering gold and rare ivory his ship carried, which had been obtained through the sale of his miserable wares.

However, on Christmas morning, while the carols rang out from shore and the church bells heralded another Christmas Day, the hand of fate set itself against the master and crew of the slaver. With a resounding crash, the vessel hit the Gilstone

Rock. The groans, curses and shrieks from the foundering ship went unheard by the people ashore, who with their carol-singing and bell-ringing were rejoicing at the arrival of Christmas. All the gold and ivory in the world could not save the captain and crew of the *Betsy Jane* as the waves of the Solway closed over her and every man on board.

Since that day, always around Christmas time, the *Betsy Jane* has been doomed to sail again and again along the Solway, whilst her captain and crew try in vain to dock her. On and on, they are doomed to sail, never to reach port.

This phenomenon is not as improbable as it might at first appear. One man I spoke to told me that on two or three occasions he, along with his wife, has observed a freak wind condition which raises a saucer-shaped area of spray off the surface of the sea, to a height of some ten to fifteen feet, with a width of up to thirty yards. He said: 'Seen at sea-level, this looks for all the world like a dismasted schooner rushing headlong before the storm.'

Perhaps one of the best known phantom ships to haunt the Solway Firth is the ghostly sailing ship *Rotterdam*, a fine vessel, loaded with passengers, which sank with the loss of all on board over a century ago. Many times since, her phantom has been seen, usually presaging a maritime disaster, rolling in the water as if out of control in a violent storm, regardless of the weather conditions at the time of the sighting. Witnesses claimed that the phantom crew could be seen leaning over the side of the ship and the screams and cries of the terrified passengers accompanied the horrifying sight!

Many years ago a ship was wrecked in the Solway through sheer malice. She contained a wedding party whose ghosts are visible on deck when the phantom ship appears. And if this were not enough, there are also tales of the sighting of two ghostly pirate ships, usually seen off Burrow Head which, on account of their many crimes, are fated to haunt the Solway Firth till Doomsday!

Many years ago, on a fine night with a harvest moon, three young reapers had been working late and having gathered in the last sheaves they walked down to the shores of the Solway. They saw two ships come sailing in. The first had neither captain nor crew aboard, only a black shadow could be seen moving about the deck which appeared to be rigging the sails and steering the ship. The other vessel had a captain, a full crew and passengers, and from her came the happy sound of music and laughter. The tide was sweeping in, high and strong, and the reapers, watching from the shore, shouted out to the crew to sail carefully. But no one took heed of the warning, save for a black dog on the prow that answered with a howl.

It was obvious to the watchers that the ships were going to dash themselves to pieces on the rocks and that all on board would be drowned. Then they would be able to row out to the wrecks where there would be barrels of wine, kegs of brandy and rich pickings from the passengers' possessions. They could take all they wanted.

Then, as if he realized what the three watchers were thinking, the black shadow on the first ship hove to. He let down a black boat with shadowy oarsmen and rowed towards the shore. The reapers ran to the water's edge, leapt into the boat, and rowed away towards the second ship, which had also hove to. Here they clambered aboard to a great sound of welcome: music and laughter. A great company gathered round them, handing out cups full of wine. But as the young men tasted the wine, the cups fell. There was a sudden shudder of dread, a cloud of darkness, the water swirled about the ships and they sank down into the swirling waters of the Solway.

No more was ever heard of the three young reapers but, according to legend, the ghostly ships still return from time to time and each time they do, they have taken a victim. The story is given credence by the occasional sighting of the rotting hulls of two ships, which occasionally appear in the quicksands before the waters of the Firth rush over them again and they disappear. They are said to be the remains of two Danish pirate ships which came to wreak havoc on the Scottish shores, only to be wrecked when the drunken crews disregarded the dangerous rocks. Some say they were led by the Devil himself!

The last ghostly tale connected with the Solway Firth – and there are enough ghost stories along its shores to fill a complete volume – concerns a ship that was wrecked within sight of Caerlaverock Castle, just off the B725 at the mouth of the River Nith, about eight miles south of Dumfries.

It was a terribly stormy night, the rain and squalls accompanied by thunder and lightning, when Will Borlan stood looking out of the window of his cottage. He saw a ship heading towards the shore, her canvas torn, masts broken and the sea foaming over her. As he watched, a flash of lightning revealed two people standing on the deck of the stricken ship: a richly attired lady 'wi a flash o' jewels aboot her', and a well-dressed gentleman, holding on to each other.

Will shouted to his son to fetch a lantern but, even before they could get their capes on, a huge wave crashed over the doomed ship and the couple were swept away into the raging water. Will and his son ran down to the shore and there they met Gilbert Gyrape, a local fisherman who had a cottage nearby. Gilbert told them that he had tried to save the couple, but they had been swept away.

But as he spoke, a giant wave swept the body of the woman ashore and as Will gently lifted her, he saw that jewels had been torn from her ears, rings had been torn from her fingers and the necklace had gone from around her neck. Although the sea had drowned her, the marks on her neck and breast, her bruised fingers and torn ears were proof that someone had robbed her of her jewellery.

The poor woman was buried in the local churchyard with due reverence, but her husband's body was never recovered. No one actually accused Gilbert to his face, but everyone suspected him of robbing the corpse. Their suspicions were confirmed when Gilbert, once a poor fisherman, suddenly prospered. He married and had children; he gave up his cottage and had a fine house built. He joined a religious sect and had hard words and sour looks for any poor folk he thought had gone astray. He gained power and riches, but little or no respect. Few would even speak to him and 'the verra beggars wouldna ask frae him'.

A few years after the shipwreck, Will and his son had gone down to the shore just as night fell to check their nets. The sea was still, there was no wind and the sky was clear. Suddenly, they heard what sounded like wings hovering over the water, and saw a light shine: a line of light, dancing and shimmering over the Solway; a light which was neither moon nor stars.

It drifted over to the shore and into Gilbert's old cottage, supposedly empty, since he had moved into his fine new house. Suddenly there was a scream of terror and three men came rushing out. Will recognized them as three of the most notorious smugglers on the coast. They came running up to him and his son.

The smugglers gasped out that they had seen the ghost of a woman in white, who stood within the bright light that came into the cottage. She was holding a golden casket close to her, as if to keep it from being taken – and there were marks on her neck and breast. Looking back at the cottage they saw that the light had now gone and the building stood in total darkness once more.

The story of the haunting soon spread. Others claimed to have seen the uncanny light and vowed that they too had seen the ghost of the woman and the bright light surrounding her. Many also remembered the shipwreck and the suspicious activities of Gilbert Gyrape. Then one evening, not long after the sighting of the ghostly woman by two more locals, a man called David Haining was riding home from the Rood Fair at Dumfries. All was quiet until he heard the sound of horses' hooves and saw a rider suddenly overtake him, fleeing with a screech of terror. He recognized the rider as Gilbert. Chasing him and about to catch up with him was a shadowy phantom 'fair fearsome tae see'! The riders rushed on and David rode home, alarmed at what had just taken place.

It is said that from that night, nothing went right for Gilbert. Crops withered in his fields and his flocks died. One by one his wife and children sickened and died, and no servants would work in his house. Then, one night, the house mysteriously caught fire and burnt to the ground. Eventually Gilbert himself went insane and was one day seen to stagger towards the shore and the sea, making a sudden rush for the water's edge. Calling out across the water, he waded in, put his hands beneath the surface and brought them out again, as if holding something.

People on the shore called out for him to come back, and even as some of them ran down to the shore to drag him back, a huge wave suddenly surged in and swept the feeble Gilbert down under the water that had drowned the lady years before. Gilbert Gyrape's body was never recovered.

The village of Achiltibuie stands some eight miles to the north-west of Ullapool, off the A835 on the shores of Baden Bay.

One August evening a touring holidaymaker arrived at the village after a long day walking the area, and was directed to a lonely guest house on an open stretch of moor, where he sought a bed for the night. Given a well-furnished room he went to bed, tired after a long day and soon fell asleep. But the next morning he arrived at the breakfast table looking pale and tired.

The tourist told his host that he had been wakened during the night by footsteps which sounded like 'the sucking of feet on the wet moors'. The footsteps were followed by a terrible crash and although he saw nothing, the man said that there was something unearthly in his room. There was a draught of cold air and a voice in the darkness said: 'I am Calum Breac. Follow me and I will show you why I have come.'

Thinking it was his host who was in some kind of trouble, the tourist got out of bed and went through the open bedroom door. He went downstairs and when he found himself at the front door he felt an ice-cold breeze, despite the fact it was a warm August night. By this time he was fully awake and he realized that the voice he had heard had not been that of his host – nor had it been human! Scared, he rushed back to his room and locked the door.

The host looked at his guest and gave him a sympathetic nod. He explained that there was a ghost in the house which took on the terrifying form of an old man with angry eyes and a black beard. He said he had seen it on a couple of occasions himself, and had no idea why it should haunt the house.

Just two months after these events, the house mysteriously burned down and the cause still remains unknown today. However, following the fire, it was noticed that the lintel above the front door bore an inscription on the inside which had been covered over, and had been a headstone probably from the long disused churchyard nearby. The inscription read: 'In memory of Calum Breac'.

The house had to be demolished after the fire and was completely rebuilt, but minus the headstone. So far as I am aware there have been no further ghostly manifestations – at least, no one will admit to any!

When Harald Hadrada, the Norse King, set out to conquer England in 1066, he was said to have been armed with a terrible weapon – a magic flag which guaranteed victory to whoever possessed it. But at Stamford Bridge the magic ran out and Harald Hadrada's army was well and truly beaten by the English King Harold, who was himself destined to die some days later at the Battle of Hastings.

Following the Battle of Stamford Bridge, the magic Norse flag vanished – or did it? The MacLeods of Dunvegan, on the Isle of Skye, trace their ancestry back to Harald Hadrada, and their most treasured heirloom is a tattered banner of faded brown silk, carefully darned in red, which is kept in the drawing room of Dunvegan Castle. It is known as Bratach Sith – or Fairy Flag – and could be the missing magic flag of Harald Hadrada.

There is an old tradition that if the MacLeods are in desperate peril, they will become invincible by unfurling the Fairy Flag in battle. But this magic will only work three times, and the clan have already used it twice. The first occasion was at Glendale in 1490, when they were fighting for their lives against the Mac-Donalds. They unfurled the flag – which by tradition is defended by twelve champion swordsmen – and the tide of the battle turned. Soon the battlefield was strewn with MacDonald dead.

The second victory was at Watermish in 1520. Again, the enemy were the MacDonalds and the MacLeods were hopelessly outnumbered. But as soon as the flag was unfurled, the Mac-Donalds were bewildered by the sight of a vast army marching down on them.

It is more than likely that the MacLeods often carried the flag into battle without unfurling it. As recently as the Second World War, many young clansmen carried its photograph as a lucky charm. When Dunvegan Castle was seriously damaged by fire in 1938, many people were convinced it was the Fairy Flag of the MacLeods which had prevented it from being destroyed completely.

The famous Fairy Bridge at Dunvegan Castle has long had an evil reputation, and for years it was said that no horse would cross it without shying.

Perhaps the most famous legend surrounding the death of Sir Francis Drake is rather like those surrounding King Arthur and other legendary warriors, who rose from their eternal slumbers when their country needed them.

When Sir Francis lay dying in 1596, on board ship off Puerto Bello, Panama, he gave orders that his drum should be sent back to Buckland Abbey, his home in Devon. He promised that if England was ever again in serious danger, and if anyone beat on the drum, he would hear its note and come at once to his country's aid.

In the course of time, this legend went through a strange alteration and, in the more modern version, the drum will roll without human agency, just before a war. Indeed, in 1914, there were rumours that it had been heard in the West Country, and there is more tangible evidence that it rolled at Scapa Flow in 1919, when the German fleet officially surrendered. A single drum was heard beating on the flagship of the Grand Fleet as the ships closed round the German vessels. Although a thorough search was made for the drummer, even while the drumroll went on, every sailor was found at his correct battle station, and there was no sign of any unauthorized drum.

The mystery remains today, but sailors are certain that it was Drake's drum, and that the admiral was with them in their final victory – just as he had always been throughout the years of the Great War.

During the seventeenth century, there lived in Badenoch, Inverness, a man who was afraid of neither man nor beast. He was a devout Christian against whose courage and honesty no evil could prevail, and he devoted his life to rooting out the witches that plagued the district.

One evening, while he was out hunting with his dogs, a terrible storm began and he was forced to take shelter in a herdsman's hut. He had just lit a fire when he heard scratching at the door. Outside was a cat with its fur bedraggled by the rain as it cowered against the wall for shelter. The kindly hunter called off his dogs and stood to one side to let the unfortunate creature into the hut. Then the cat spoke to him and said it was a witch and had come to the hunter to beg for mercy, and for help in mending its wicked ways. The hunter was naive enough to believe it at first, bidding the cat to come in and warm itself. But the cat still hesitated: 'First tie your dogs to that beam,' it said. 'And here is a long grey hair to tie them with.' Now the hunter became suspicious of the witch and, pretending to do as he was told, fastened only one end round the beam, leaving his dogs free.

The cat settled by the fire and at once began to grow bigger. It grew to the size of a calf, then suddenly, a woman stood before the astonished hunter. To his horror, he recognized her; she was a neighbour from his village, a woman so virtuous she was known as the 'Goodwife of Laggan'.

'Hunter of the hills', she hissed, 'your hour has come. I drowned our greatest persecutor at Raasay this morning and now it is your turn.' With her fingers hooked, she flew at the hunter's throat. The dogs leapt at her, tearing her breast and side. Unable to beat them off, the witch changed herself into a blackbird and flew out of the door.

Arriving home some hours later, the hunter found his wife and neighbours anxiously gathered at the bedside of the Goodwife of Laggan. They told him how she had gone out to gather peat, and had returned home gravely ill. In reply, the hunter stripped off the bedclothes and revealed the terrible wounds on the woman's body. He recounted what had happened and the villagers seized the witch and hanged her from the nearest tree.

A superstitious legend? Perhaps. But before dismissing it, consider the experience of the two travellers on the Badenoch road several years ago, who were terrified by the bloody apparition of a woman rushing past them, with two big black dogs in pursuit. Shortly after, a rider appeared on a black horse and when the travellers told him what they had seen, the rider asked: 'Would the dogs have caught her before she reached Dalarossie churchyard?' The men thought it likely and on hearing this, the horseman laughed and rode on.

A few minutes later, the travellers heard shrieking behind them and turned to see the black horseman gallop by at an incredible speed. Across the saddle was slung the screaming woman, and the big black hounds continued to leap up and tear at her. Had they witnessed the ghost of the Goodwife of Laggan trying to reach the sanctuary of Dalarossie churchyard? If that was so, then it is not difficult to imagine who the dark man was that prevented her from doing so.

In my part of the country, we like to paraphrase Shakespeare: 'The bad they did, lives after them. The good they interred with their bones.' This is certainly the case with regard to Tam Dalyell – or the 'Muscovy brute', as he was known – the general of the Royalist forces during the wars that virtually destroyed Scotland in the seventeenth century. He is still known by the Scots as the 'Muscovy brute', as he was the man thought to have introduced the thumbscrews into Scotland from Russia.

A man of great military prowess, Tam Dalyell was feared and

detested by the Covenanters, who swore he owed his success to the Devil. Something which was made all the more believable when he built his home, 'The Binns', near Blackness – just off the B903, north of Linlithgow – with round towers to prevent the Devil from blowing the house away.

Today, the house is owned and run by the National Trust for Scotland, and among the many relics to be seen here are the cards, goblet, spoon and table, which are said to have figured largely in his gallivantings with the Devil, Tam's boots can also be seen which, you will be solemnly told, disappear occasionally, when his ghost borrows them to ride around the districts.

There are many tales told of his dealings with the Devil, but the most popular tells of their famous card game which Tam won. The Devil, always a bad loser, picked up the marble table in his rage and flung it at Dalyell's head. Tam ducked and it sailed through the window to land in Sergeant's Pond, at the foot of Binns Hill. This particular legend was borne out in 1878 when the pond was being cleaned out, and the table was found there. Today it has been restored to the house and can be seen by visitors. Also to be seen on occasion is Tam's ghost, mounted on a white horse and usually seen in the vicinity of the old road which leads up to the house.

Until the nineteenth century, there was a village near Stenton, on the B6370 south-west of Dunbar, called Whittingehame. All that is left to remind us of the village are the remains of Whittinge-hame Castle, just outside Stenton.

For many years, the area was said to have been haunted by the ghost of an unbaptized child. Its problem appears to be that it had no name and therefore could not identify itself in the next world. No villager dared approach the unhappy creature, let alone talk to it, until a drunkard, reeling home one night, saw it and cried out to the phantom: 'How's a' this morning, Short-hoggers?' Immediately, the ghostly child rushed off joyfully shouting: 'They ca' me Short-hoggers o' Whittingehame!' He was never seen again.

Short-hoggers is a Scots name for footless socks (similar to modern-day leg-warmers), which people thought to be an apt name considering the number of years the spirit had wandered the district!

A rather strange occurrence took place at Mellon Udrigle, near Laide, at the beginning of the nineteenth century, which has never been explained.

It appears that the menfolk of Mellon Udrigle were attending a service at Clachan Church but, because of the distance involved, most of the women had been left at home. Before the day was out, however, they began to wish that they had undertaken the long journey with their menfolk.

During the course of the day, the whole sea between Black Island and Priest Island suddenly filled with naval vessels. For the women spectators, it was, at first, a moment of breathless excitement as they came running from their homes to gather in a noisy, chattering group to watch as the men-of-war and galleys, filled with soldiers and arms, speedily rowed to the shore.

Then, some of the women began to feel frightened, for the reputation of the English soldiers was not a good one in these parts, especially when one remembered some of the horrifying stories told concerning their exploits during the '45 Rebellion. The young girls of the village were hastily gathered together and told to take cover on nearby Greenstone Point, whilst the older women returned to their homes to quickly collect their valuables and jewellery and bury them deep in the sandy soil.

For some considerable time, the frightened women watched the soldiers rowing towards the shore – but strange to relate, no boat got that far, and no soldier or sailor ever landed. Although there have been claims in subsequent years of phantom ships in the area, the whole incident remains a complete mystery. However, it is suggested that when, in 1914, the Grand Fleet under Lord Jellicoe concentrated on using a number of the western lochs as secret bases, for reasons which are best left alone, Loch Ewe was hastily abandoned. Locals believe that the vision at Mellon Udrigle was the forerunner of scenes to come.

Several years ago, two friends, a Mrs Wallace and Miss Fraser, rented an old mansion in central Scotland for their summer holiday.

One day, the weather being too bad for walking, Mrs Wallace went to explore the outbuildings and came to a room which had once been the wash-house. Here she was startled to hear a strange noise coming from an old copper boiler. When she went to peer inside it, expecting to find a rat, Mrs Wallace was surprised to find herself looking down, not into a boiler, but a deep well – at the bottom of which she could distinctly see the figure of a man!

She was able to make him out quite clearly because he seemed to be lit by a weird light which appeared to emanate from inside him. He was dressed in what appeared to be a quilted flowery dressing gown and was bending over a box, which he was trying his best to conceal under a pile of rubbish. Satisfied the box was well hidden, the man stood up and looked upwards into the frightened face of Mrs Wallace; the look of evil joy on his own face changing to one of diabolical fury as their eyes met. Suddenly the man leapt upwards and began to climb up the wall of the well with the assuredness of a spider. Needless to say, the poor woman fled in terror.

A few nights later, matters came to a climax when Mrs Wallace suddenly realized her bedroom was haunted. She was half asleep in the semi-darkened room when suddenly an enormous cat, its tail upright, stalked over her legs before perching on the bedrail at her feet, fixing her with a malevolent stare.

Then, to her horror, in the corner by the chimney, she saw the man who had been in the well and he appeared to be holding a baby. The man was scowling at the child, his scowl suddenly changing to a look of fury and then, gnashing his teeth and stamping his feet in anger, he lifted the baby up and dropped it head first into the fire. The now terrified Mrs Wallace watched it as it seemed to fall in slow motion; she heard the dull thud as it landed in the fire and heard it burn as she screamed out in terror. Then, dropping the heavy poker with which he had been holding the baby down in the flames, the man turned and looked at her with a hellish expression on his face.

Mrs Wallace screamed again at this and, hearing the approach of Miss Fraser, the man appeared to give a signal to the cat, which sprang at her throat. This was just too much for Mrs Wallace who promptly fainted. When she came to, some minutes later, the room was empty, save for Miss Fraser who was convinced her friend had suffered a nightmare.

Even today and despite investigation by the Society for Psychical Research, the events have never been fully explained.

# 3   Tenements of Terror

It is a dark, stormy night but you are safe in bed – or so you think. Suddenly the air turns ice cold, your dog howls and a ghostly figure walks through the wall. You are being haunted. But you are not alone; it can happen to anyone at any time.

In the mid-1970s, two young women students, studying at Dundee University, were fortunate enough to find a small flat in an old tenement building in nearby Morgan Street. Here they shared a tiny living-room-cum-kitchen, bathroom and bedroom, and for some time life was fun. Both girls enjoyed their studies, they got on well together and they found life at the university exciting.

Then, one morning, things began to go wrong. One of the girls who had no lectures to attend until the afternoon, woke up to find her flatmate looking down at her with a strange expression on her face. The flatmate asked her drowsy friend if she felt all right. Without waiting for an answer, she said she was late for her lecture but would explain later and with that she left hurriedly.

Over their meal later in the day, the flatmate explained her strange behaviour. She said that on the previous night she had been unable to sleep and at about 3.30 in the morning, the hall light had suddenly snapped on. Then she heard someone moving about in the bathroom: someone with slow, padding steps, the sound of which terrified her, although logic told her that as the door was securely locked, no one could possibly have got into the flat.

Frightened, she had hidden under the bedclothes, but after a few minutes she took a grip on herself and she emerged again to discover the hall light was now turned off. However, she glanced across to her friend's bed and was horrified to see what she took to be an elderly woman with short grey hair, dressed in a pale blue dress, standing beside the bed apparently deep in conversation with her. Momentarily she closed her eyes and when she looked again, the figure was gone.

About a week later, one of the girls was lying in bed, round about midnight, reading as she waited for her flatmate to finish in the bathroom. Gradually she became aware that someone was moving about in the kitchen. Immediately she felt frightened, particularly as she could hear her flatmate in the bathroom. Nervously she tapped on the wall that divided the kitchen from the bedroom, and suddenly there came a terrible outburst, as if someone with superhuman strength and steel talons was trying to claw a way through the brickwork. Frantically she called the flatmate, who dashed in from the bathroom, and almost at the same time the terrifying sounds stopped, leaving the air laden with a heavy ominous silence.

Both girls were by now half scared to death and they sat together on one of the beds, clutching each other and struggling to hold back the panic that had now engulfed them. Then the savage clawing on the wall began again, this time with demonic ferocity, as if whatever was doing it was determined to smash its way through. This frenzied battering continued for nearly half an hour until, the girls' nerves suddenly snapped, and pulling on a few clothes they prepared to dash from the building, despite the fact it was so late at night.

Then, to their horror, they realized that the flat door was locked and the keys were in the living room – the very room that was occupied by something terrifyingly dreadful. But not wishing to stay where they were, they plucked up every ounce of courage they possessed and raced into the hall, flicking on the living-room light. To add to their horror, the bulb had blown and the light didn't come on. Scrabbling in a panic now, they managed to find the key and got out of the flat as quickly as they could, spending what was left of the night with some fellow students who lived on nearby Cowgate.

The following day, accompanied by several other students, the girls were able to pick up enough courage to return to the flat for their belongings. However, to the amazement of the two girls, and to add to the disbelief of their friends, they discovered that the wall between the living-room and the bedroom, despite the frenzied clawing they had both heard the night before, had not the slightest mark or tear on the wallpaper!

To this day, no one knows who or what terrified the two girls that night. As for them, they never wanted to find out. All they wanted to do was to find new accommodation as soon as possible, refusing point blank to spend one more night there.

Until her marriage, Mrs Davidson lived with her mother and three brothers and sisters in a tenement flat in Princes Street in the older part of Aberdeen.

She told me: 'The house was built between about 1807 and 1810, probably for a well-to-do merchant, and even as late as the 1881 census, it was only occupied by one family. Later the area became downgraded and most of the houses were converted to tenements for tailors, clerks, masons and various mill-workers and their families.'

For a number of years the flat was occupied by Mrs Davidson's grandfather and two aunts and, when they died, her mother and the four children took it over. It must have been quite crowded by then as it only consisted of three rooms: a kitchen and two other rooms which were in use as bedrooms.

'One day', she continued, 'I suddenly saw the dark figure of a man wearing a black cloak and a black hat, which I can only describe as looking like the figure on a bottle of Sandeman's Port. I couldn't see his face as it was lost in the shadow of the large brim of his hat.'

She said that even though she was only a young girl at the time, she was not in the least afraid of him. Quite often after that, she would catch sight of him peeping round a door at her, or just standing looking at her. The first time she saw him she told her mother who, in her typical no-nonsense way, told her that it was only a shadow caused by the darkened room. 'So, as nobody else spoke about it, for a time I believed her,' she said.

Over the years the family grew up and left home and when her brother married, he and his new bride lived with Mrs Davidson and her mother in the flat for a short time. His wife was terrified when she saw the mysterious cloaked figure but, when she too mentioned it, she received the same reply from her mother-in-law.

Mrs Davidson said: 'As I grew up I often saw "him" and once I spoke to the figure but he never replied, he simply disappeared only to reappear again a short time later. Then slowly, over a period of time, his appearances became less frequent, until he was never seen again. While we lived there I never mentioned the figure to my mother, but I couldn't help wondering about his sudden departure.'

It was only after they had moved out, some six years before her mother died, that the subject of the cloaked figure was brought up during a discussion about ghosts. Mrs Davidson said: 'Only then did my mother admit to knowing about it, describing it just as I had seen it, but saying she had refused to talk about it in the past, for fear of frightening the children.'

Her mother said that one day she was polishing a mirror and, looking through it, she saw the dark figure of a man in a cloak, wearing a wide-brimmed hat, gazing at her intently. She was not afraid, but turned to face the figure and said in a firm voice: 'I don't think you belong here. I think you should go away to where you do belong; the children here are frightened of you!'

'Which,' concluded Mrs Davidson, 'is probably why I never saw him again; our friendly ghost.'

Still in Aberdeen, comes a story from Mrs Christina George who, until about eighteen years ago, worked for a firm of contract cleaners in the city.

She told me: 'One day, a neighbour who worked for the same firm, and myself were sent to an old house in Queens Road, in the west end of Aberdeen, just across from Harlaw Park. The old house had a good number of rooms which were being converted into offices for various professional companies.'

Workmen were still finishing off the renovations in the former kitchens on the ground floor, and one of Mrs George's last jobs was to put liquid polish on the staircase, going down backwards one step at a time from the top floor of the house to the hall. She continued: 'I came to one room and looking through the doorway saw some of the workmen were still finishing off. As they were busy I didn't want to disturb them, so I had to leave off what I was doing, letting the stairs I had already polished, dry off.'

In the hallway, Mrs George saw some steps leading down to what appeared to be basement offices, in what had originally been the old cellars. So, with cloth in hand, she decided to give these steps a rub, even though this was not part of the contract. She went on: 'There were perhaps a dozen steps which spiralled down and when I reached the bottom I saw to my right, what appeared to be a newly cemented passage, with windows on the right-hand side, and a number of doors facing them. To my immediate left was another door.'

Waiting for the steps to dry, Mrs George took a couple of steps towards the door on the left to have a look at what she thought was a newly renovated office. 'I had half turned and was just about to reach for the door handle, when I felt the presence of someone in the passage. My first thought was that it was another workman, but when I turned there was no one there, yet I could hear someone shuffling towards me, someone who seemed to be having great difficulty in walking,' she said.

Suddenly, rooted to the spot in terror and overcome with a sense of evil and danger as the invisible force shuffled nearer, panic set in and she rushed up the stairs not daring to look back.

Once more in the comparative safety of the kitchen and in the company of the workmen, she sat trembling with fright, when one of the workmen came over to her and said: 'I know where you've been, lassie! We put our young sparks down there to check the wiring and he came up in a far worse state than you!'

Mrs George told me that until then she had never believed in ghosts, but now she does, and she will never forget the feeling of evil and terror in that cellar, whatever it was. So far, no one has been able to come up with a satisfactory explanation, and my own research has revealed that, up to the time of writing at least, the people who now work there have had no similar experiences.

The Grampian Transport Depot in King Street, Aberdeen, is a grim fortress-like building which, from about 1861 until the First World War, was a militia barracks. Although taken over by the Aberdeen Corporation in 1914, the barracks were still occupied by the Gordon Highlanders at the time war broke out.

At that time it housed, among other things, an officers' mess and administration block; places that are relegated as 'no-go' areas by certain members of the transport staff. For today the spirit of a long dead Army officer – a Captain Beaton – who hanged himself prior to the Gordon Highlanders embarking for France, is said to be scaring some of them half to death. Over the past few years the captain's ghost has been sighted frequently, drifting through the building in regimental dress.

One female employee told how she heard tapping on her

office window as she worked late one evening. Opening the blinds, she was unable to see anyone outside in the semi-darkness, but reflected in the glass she could see the outline of a handsome young man standing directly behind her, dressed in military uniform. She said the room went very, very cold, although at the time she did not feel frightened or threatened in any way.

A few evenings later, the same woman had another, more frightening experience. She said: 'I thought someone was playing a trick on me at first, after hearing of my previous experience.' Far away in the distance she could hear the weird tapping sound on the glass, which seemed to come nearer and nearer. No one answered when she called out and as the knocking became more urgent, she left the office to find someone else in the building. She said that the lights in the corridor were off when she left her office, but when she returned a few moments later with another employee, every light had mysteriously switched on.

The officer's ghostly figure was sighted recently, floating along one of the depot passageways and a man, sitting alone in the canteen, got the shock of his life when some invisible being blew down the back of his neck. Lights are often interfered with and more than one driver has been frightened, after being tripped up by some invisible presence.

Grampian Transport's marketing manager, Dave MacDairmaid, told me: 'Quite often, for no apparent reason, a deathly cold will descend on a number of offices. Nearly everyone here knows of the ghost and quite a few have had some experience of it. One man recently claimed to have seen a pair of feet with Highlander's spats, walking up the stairs – nothing else, just a pair of feet!'

Just after the Second World War, Mrs Annie McLennon, of Fyvie, was the landlady of a large old Victorian tenement in Edinburgh. On the fourth floor was a vacant furnished flat and she had called in a couple of men to decorate it, prior to re-letting.

She said: 'One morning, one of the decorators had come downstairs to ask if I would make them a brew of tea for their mid-morning break, leaving his partner upstairs in the bathroom of the flat, where he was on his hands and knees wiping some paint up which he had spilled on the lino.'

As he worked, the painter heard what he later described as 'the sound of bare feet' walking lightly along the passage from the bed-sitting-room. He could hear the 'sticky-tacky' sound of each foot being lifted from the linoleum. Despite the fact that he thought he was alone on the fourth floor, he did not see any reason why someone else should not be up there and he took little notice. Then, as he backed through the bathroom doorway, still on his hands and knees, the footsteps came up alongside him, and he was immediately struck by what felt like a powerful electric shock. There was a blinding flash of brilliant light and his body was momentarily stunned by a violent spasm. He staggered to his feet and still dazed, lurched towards the bed-sitting-room to sit down and recover. As he approached the door, the handle suddenly moved downwards and the door opened of its own accord!

In his confused state this barely registered, he stumbled inside and sat on the bed for a few moments, unsure of whether it was he who had closed the door again, or not.

After a minute or two, the painter returned to the job in hand wondering what had caused the startling incident. There were no electric wires or electrical equipment near where he had been working, so an ordinary electric shock could be ruled out. It was a rather nervous painter who returned to the bathroom to kneel and complete cleaning up the floor.

Instantly, there came the same flash and the electric shock, only this time it was not quite so powerful. As he stood up again totally amazed and bewildered, he was overcome by a feeling of inexplicable grief; a feeling that came from nowhere and for no reason, yet it brought him close to tears.

Mrs McLennon said: 'Just at that moment his mate returned with a tray of tea I had made for them both. Seeing his partner in an obvious state of shock and depression, he asked what the matter was. When he was told that the bathroom was probably haunted, the reaction was immediate. The man carrying the tray dropped it down the stairwell, where it crashed on the floor of the hall four storeys below.'

The reason for the man's reaction was that while she was making the tea, Mrs McLennon had told him that the flat they were working on was being redecorated because three weeks earlier, the tenant, a young woman, had committed suicide by hanging herself from the bathroom door by her dressing gown cord. She had done this after her fiancé had broken off their engagement. 'Tenants never seemed to stay very long in that flat after that,' Mrs McLennon concluded.

One of Scotland's best-known hauntings took place in the home of Andrew Mackie and his family at Galloway. The strange events which took place there in 1698 were fully authenticated in a report published at the time which was certified by several ministers, local lairds and other people of repute who were eyewitnesses to the remarkable events which have remained unexplained for three centuries.

It all began one night when Mackie discovered his cattle had been let out of the cowshed. The same thing happened again the next night but, on this occasion, Mackie discovered one of his cows tied to an overhead beam, its hooves inches above ground!

On another occasion, a quantity of peat was found to have been brought into the house and for several days after, stones were quite inexplicably thrown about the place. Then someone noticed that although the stones were mostly thrown at night, they never appeared to be thrown on the Sabbath. A blanket and stool were discovered, formed into the shape resembling that of a person; pot hooks and hangers disappeared, only to be found a few days later in places which had already been searched.

After several weeks, there was more stone throwing, more frequent than before, even on the Sabbath and especially when the members of the household were gathered together in prayer. After a further month or two, these disturbances suddenly stopped, and the family began to think that their troubles were over – in fact, they had only just begun. Within a week stones were being thrown again, but this time they were much more damaging, causing pain and bruising to anyone unfortunate enough to be on the receiving end of one. A stout stick was wielded as if by an invisible being, which hit several witnesses around the head and shoulders.

People in bed were disturbed by loud raps and knocks on doors and furniture, and things soon became so bad that several servants refused to stay in the house a moment longer. Andrew Mackie was himself hit about the forehead or pushed from behind, sometimes accompanied by a sharp scratch to his scalp. At other times he was dragged across the room by his clothes, something which was later experienced by the local miller who visited the house, full of scorn and convinced that the phenomena were all in the mind. He soon changed his opinion when an invisible force dragged him screaming around the room before roughly depositing him in a corner.

The children had their bedclothes ripped off their beds and were severely beaten about the legs. The slaps were so loud it sounded as if they were being beaten by a heavy man and could be heard all through the house. At the same time, various objects were seen by several witnesses, moving about the house of their own accord.

But by far the most sinister was a rough voice which was heard during family prayers, repeating over and over: 'Hush! Hush!' Each time the family dog heard the unfamiliar voice, it would give a yelp, as if it had been kicked, and then bolted for the door. If it was possible, things became even worse. Groaning and whistling was heard, mysterious fires were started, with lumps of burning peat being thrown at the family. Fireballs fell both inside and outside the house, vanishing as soon as they touched the ground. Very hot stones were discovered in the children's beds, too hot even to handle after several hours on the stone floor.

At the time these events took place, the house was less than thirty years old and a local magistrate arranged to examine every person who had been in any way associated with it during this period. As the enquiry progressed, it was revealed that, during the construction, human remains had been discovered on the site, which suggested that a murder had been committed and the victim buried there.

Sir Alexander Seton, tenth Baronet of Abercorn and Armour Bearer to the Queen, lived in Learmont Gardens, Edinburgh, the scene of many strange and weird incidents which appear to have centred around the bone of an ancient Egyptian, given to the first Lady Seton on a visit to the Temple of Luxor in 1936.

One night, shortly after their arrival back at Learmont Gardens, Sir Alexander showed the bone to some friends when, following dinner, they were discussing their recent trip to Egypt and its many fascinating mysteries. With mock dignity, Sir Alexander deposited the relic in a glass case, ceremoniously placing it on a small table in one corner of the dining-room. Almost at once, strange things began to occur, until Sir

Alexander was firmly convinced that he was cursed for having the wretched thing in his possession.

That same night – just as his dinner guests were about to leave, in fact – there was a terrific crash and a large piece of the roof parapet smashed to the ground, missing Sir Alexander by mere inches. Next morning it was discovered that a chimney pot had also fallen to the ground although, later, Sir Alexander did admit that this may have been pure coincidence, as it had been a rather windy night.

Several nights later, the children's nanny burst into Sir Alexander's bedroom, saying that she could hear someone moving about in the dining-room downstairs. He immediately got out of bed to investigate, but he could find nothing to account for the sounds, and nothing appeared to be out of place. Back in bed, he himself heard a heavy crash and the following morning, Lady Seton angrily accused him of upsetting the corner table, which she had found lying on its side, with the glass case containing the bone lying nearby on the floor.

A few weeks after this event, a nephew, Alistair Black, came to stay at Learmont Gardens, and he calmly announced at the breakfast table one morning, that he had gone to the bathroom during the night and had seen a person 'in a very funny looking garb', going up the stairs. Soon, other visitors and members of the staff also claimed to have seen the robed spectral figure, wandering about the house at night.

As a result of this and other uncanny events, Sir Alexander decided to keep watch on the bone, which now rested in the upstairs drawing-room. One night, he very carefully locked the doors and windows and kept watch from the balcony outside. For several hours he waited in the cold Edinburgh night air and, as nothing happened, he decided to call the whole thing off and went back to his warm bed. He had just fallen asleep, when he was rudely awakened by his wife, who said she could hear someone walking about in the dining-room. Picking up his pistol, Sir Alexander went once more to investigate, meeting in the passageway a frightened nanny, who had also heard the noises clearly emanating from the locked room.

Quietly unlocking the door and throwing it open, Sir Alexander was met with a scene of total devastation. Chairs had been overturned, books thrown about, furniture had been moved and a priceless antique vase had been smashed to smithereens. Yet alone, and untouched in the midst of all this mayhem, remained the Egyptian relic. The windows were still locked and there was no way in which a human could have entered the room.

Over the next few weeks, apart from two unaccountable fires, a few bangs and other inexplicable noises, the house was reasonably quiet, until one night when they were all kept awake by loud crashes coming from the dining-room, which sounded as if the house was being systematically wrecked. Eventually it was decided to move most of the transportable articles down to the sitting-room, leaving only the heaviest furniture in the drawing-room. The glass case containing the bone was also removed to the sitting-room.

A couple of days later, this room also was found to be in a terrible mess, with articles thrown about, furniture overturned, vases and expensive ornaments smashed, glassware smashed inside cabinets and nothing left untouched – except the glass case containing the Egyptian relic.

Needless to say the press soon got to know of the strange happenings at Learmont Gardens and headlines such as: 'BARONET FEARS PHARAOH CURSE ON FAMILY' began to appear across Scotland. One intrepid and sceptical journalist asked if he could borrow the bone for a few days. He returned it after three days, saying nothing had happened, and he wrote a scathing article for his newspaper in which he poured scorn on the so-called 'curse'. A week later the same reporter became quite ill and had to have emergency surgery for a burst appendix!

Meanwhile, the troublesome bone had been returned to the upstairs drawing-room, and one night when the family nanny was alone in the house, she heard another terrific crash. Too afraid to investigate, she waited until Sir Alexander returned home and he, on being told, went straight upstairs to investigate. He found the drawing-room undisturbed, but for the bone and the table on which it stood. The table lay on its side, smashed – and the bone, now broken into several pieces, lay beside it.

This was the last straw. Sir Alexander decided to get rid of the horrible thing, but Lady Seton would not hear of it. She took the bone to a doctor friend and asked him if he would repair it as best he could. Afterwards it was placed on a table in the hall at the doctor's residence until one day, his maid, running in terror from a mysterious robed figure, fell over the table and broke her leg! The doctor wasted no time in returning it to the Setons.

One evening, a few weeks after the return of the relic, the Setons were holding a small dinner party, during which time the bone suddenly hurled itself and the table on which it stood across the dining room, hitting the opposite wall with a resounding crash and causing the dinner party to break up in uproar. Now, Sir Alexander decided that, whether his wife agreed or not, the bone was going.

He had an uncle who was Father Benedict of the Abbey of Fort Augustus, and it was arranged that the monk would come to Learmont Gardens, unknown to Lady Seton, to exorcise the evil object. The ceremony took place while she and the children were away on holiday and the relic, after exorcism, was destroyed by burning. What was left was put into a bucket and thrown out with the ashes.

But the curse did not end with the destruction of the bone. From that day, until his death in 1962, trouble always seemed to beset Sir Alexander. When he died, shortly after marrying for the third time, he was still convinced in the belief that robbing an Egyptian tomb had brought down the 'Curse of the Pharaohs' on the heads of those who had been responsible for its violation.

The ghosts of Ballechin House, near Dunkeld, some ten miles to the north-west of Perth on the A9, have not acquired anything like the fame of their spectral counterparts in other areas of Scotland. Yet this haunting was in many ways a far better one than most, perhaps more accurately observed and authenticated than even the famous hauntings at Borley Rectory in Essex.

Here, there was everything a good haunting should have – house guests freezing with cold and fear in a lonely Highland mansion, ghostly nuns weeping by a frozen burn, spectral tattoos of a fearful nature, the disembodied paws of a dog; to mention but a few of the unexplained phenomena which, over the years, have chilled the spines of the people who stayed at Ballechin.

The house has been the source of controversy since the death of Major Robert Steuart in 1876 and there is still considerable discussion surrounding the hauntings today. In 1892, a Jesuit priest complained of loud and inexplicable noises, while sleeping in one of the rooms. Even after he had changed his room the loud noises seemed to follow him; one of them being something which sounded like some large dog throwing itself violently against the bottom of the bedroom door. He also claimed to have heard raps and bangs, followed by a loud shriek.

When John Steuart – the newphew of Major Robert – inherited the house, he reported seeing a procession of monks and nuns, when he looked out of the window one evening. The following day he left for a visit to London and met a sudden death, when he was run over and killed by a cab in a busy London street.

A former governess of Ballechin left because there were so many queer noises which seemed to follow her about the house. In the late 1890s, the house was let to a family for twelve months and they left after just a few weeks, forfeiting the remainder of the rent, rather than suffer the fearful rattling, knocking, thumping against doors, footsteps and other weird phenomena which they were unable to explain.

Bedding was torn from beds, the rustle of silk was heard, as if a woman was crossing the room, groans accompanied by fearful knockings and heavy breathing, which were all usually preceded by an icy chill.

The daughter of the tenant, terrified at the sound of a man limping around her bed, called in her brother who then slept on the sofa. The limping began again and he heard it also – yet neither of them could see anyone. Later the brother claimed to have seen the ghost of a limping man on two separate occasions – once in the form of an indeterminate mist, and once in the shape of a man who came in by the door and vanished after limping across the room and walking through a wall. It is interesting to learn that Major Robert Steuart walked with a limp, which he gained during his army career in India.

Ballechin House finally went out of the Steuarts' possession. In 1932 it was bought by Mr Wemyss Honeyman, who still owned the estate as late as 1970. In later years, the house remained uninhabited for a long time – by the denizens of this world at any rate. Its end came in 1963, when, like its more famous counterpart at Borley, it was demolished.

Two writers who have influenced me over the years, have been W.T. Stead and Catherine Crowe. But like many Victorian writers on the supernatural, they had the most infuriating habit of rarely giving the name of the person they were discussing. Regular readers of ghost literature will no doubt have discovered this and, like me, find it annoying. One cannot help wondering why Mr P— of S— Street, in the town of M—, was afraid to make himself known; or was it just that the author wished to spare the blushes of the townsfolk, yet at the same time assure readers that the person really existed?

In her *Night Side of Nature*, first published in 1848, Mrs Crowe tells us the story concerning Mr C. S—, who lived for many years at A— House in Scotland. It doesn't take a lot of research to discover that this refers to Mr Charles Kirkpatrick Sharpe, who lived for many years at Allanbank House, the grim, imposing former seat of the Stuarts and haunted by the ghost of 'Pearlin Jean', whose persistent hauntings were so thoroughly believed and established as to leave us in no doubt as to their authenticity.

Pearlin Jean was so called because whenever she appeared, she always wore 'pearlins' – the Scots name for a certain type of lace. She was a Frenchwoman whom Robert Stuart, the first Baronet Allanbank, met in Paris during his tour to finish his education as a gentleman, sometime during the 1670s. There are those who argue that she was a nun, in which case she would almost certainly have been a Sister of Charity; otherwise, at that time, she would have been confined to a cloister.

Whoever she was, she and Robert fell in love. But it would appear that his parents disapproved of the relationship and he was called home to Scotland. He had climbed into his carriage for his return journey home when Jeanne ran up to him and implored him to stay. As she stepped on the front wheel of his carriage to plead with him, he ordered the coachman to drive on, the consequence of which was that the young woman fell, and one of the coach wheels ran over her head, killing her instantly.

Just over a week later, on a dusky autumn evening, Robert Stuart arrived home. As he drove under the arched gateway at Allanbank, the horses gave a frightened neigh and suddenly reared. The coachman lashed out at them with his whip, but both horses stood fixed to the spot, their eyes rolling with fear.

Stuart looked out of the coach and an unfamiliar object caught his eye; something white and red perched on top of the gateway. He stared, his face drained of blood, at the rich lace skirts moving softly in the breeze, as the ghost of Jeanne stretched out her arms to him in welcome, bending her head, from which the blood streamed on to her white shoulders and bodice.

Robert Stuart was never the same man after that, nor was Allanbank – where nothing more eventful usually happened than the occasional domestic birth or death – the same place. Now it became a place to be feared. Unaccountable things happened at night. Doors opened and shut with a great noise, usually around midnight; a hideous scream was often heard, which was enough to chill the blood; and the rustling of silks accompanied by the patter of high heels was heard in rooms and passages.

In later years, Charles Kirkpatrick Sharpe reported how his old nurse, Jenny Blackadder, often heard Pearlin Jean rustling in silks up and down stairs and along the passage. The housekeeper, Bettie Norris, frequently saw the ghost and became so used to her, that she was no longer frightened either of her noises, or of seeing her.

Many years later, two ladies paid a visit to Allanbank and spent one night there. They knew nothing of the ghost, but the next morning they left hurriedly after complaining of being disturbed all the previous night by something which walked to and fro across their bedroom.

Pearlin Jean's ghost was last seen around the turn of the century, although she had been heard quite often until about fifty years ago. By then her powers seemed to be failing and she was regarded more with affection than fear. But then, time, like ivy, creeps over the memory of all wrongs – even the cruel one that had been done to poor Pearlin Jean.

Mrs Anne Smith of Aberdeen told me an interesting story concerning a house she moved into with her parents in the town, in 1951, where events began even before the furniture was moved in.

She told me: 'Just prior to moving in, my father made me go down to the house to wash all the floors before the carpets were laid. It was a fairly large house and right from the very first day I felt that there was some kind of presence upstairs. In fact, after the first day when I was there on my own, I pleaded with my mother not to make me go again. But my father was very strict and a non-believer in ghosts or anything of that nature so, scared as I was, I had to keep going back alone to the house to finish the job.'

However, although the house had some form of atmosphere about it and was, according to Anne, 'rather creepy sometimes', it was not until about 1958 that the apparition began to manifest itself. Anne said: 'One night, I was frightened when a white form floated into my bedroom and stood at the foot of my bed for a few seconds, before floating out again.'

Although Anne's mother didn't see it, she heard the ghost on several occasions. Once, alone in the house with only the family dog for company, she heard someone run downstairs, cross the hall and disappear into a room at the bottom of the staircase. Apparently the dog went berserk, its fur standing on end, growling and snarling at something unseen.

'On another occasion, I had gone to bed, my dad was out, and my mother heard someone moving about in the hall,' Anne continued. 'She thought it was me moving about and called out to ask what I was up to. When I didn't reply, she came up to my bedroom and found me fast asleep.' She later learned that when there was no one in the house, her mother would never go upstairs if she could help it.

Anne Smith married and moved out of the house but, early in the 1970s, she and her children visited her parents on Christmas Day. Two young nieces were also there and as they and Anne's two sons played in the hall, 'capering about with the lights out', they were suddenly frightened by what they described as 'a white man' on the stairs. On another occasion, when the children were staying with their grandparents and sleeping in what was once their mother's room, they ran downstairs screaming and saying there was a man standing by the window in their room.

It appears that, prior to Anne's parents buying the house, a previous occupant had lived in it alone for several years and he had been found dead in bed – in the room where Anne Smith used to sleep. Apparently his ghost has also been seen walking in the street outside.

Inverawe House is situated at Taynuilt in the rugged Pass of Brander, overlooked by Ben Cruachan. It is a typical Scottish manor house and home of the Campbells, who have been associated with it for over four hundred years. It seems that the first Inverawe was the son of Sir Neil of Lochow, who died in the early fourteenth century and who had married the sister of Robert the Bruce. The family is probably the oldest branch of Argyll to still hold the Campbell name.

For a number of years now, the ghost of a woman has been seen in the Ticonderoga room. She is known as 'Green Jean', as her true identity is somewhat obscure, although some disputed evidence suggests she may be the Maid of Collard.

In 1912, on the night before new owners moved in to Inverawe, loud screams were heard coming from the empty Ticonderoga room. The disturbance was thought to have been caused by Green Jean finding the room empty of all accustomed furniture.

During the 1940s, a guest staying at the house was putting up his fishing rod. Glancing up to check the top of his rod, he saw, to his amazement, the slim figure of a girl in a green dress walking along the gallery which overlooked the main hall. She had long fair hair, an attractive face, and looked to be no more than about fifteen or sixteen years old. Reaching the end of the gallery, the mysterious figure then disappeared into the Ticonderoga room and was not seen again.

It seems that Green Jean has been fairly quiet over the past few years, although at least one guest has been made aware of her presence, for in the summer of 1967, when he was sleeping in the Ticonderoga room, the ghostly girl turned him over in bed! Apparently, according to legend, the ghost only appeared to members of the Clan Campbell – and the guest's name was Campbell.

Another ghost associated with Inverawe House goes back to the early eighteenth century, when Donald Campbell came face to face with his sworn enemy, Stewart of Appin. Both men immediately drew their swords and there was a bitter fight to the death. Stewart won, and as he stood wiping the blood from his sword, he saw the body of Donald Campbell floating down the river into which it had fallen. Knowing that it was only a matter of time before the Campbells would find it and come howling for his blood, Stewart decided to rely on the ancient law of Highland hospitality, whereby any man could always consider himself safe while being entertained under the roof of a Highland house.

So, he set off for Inverawe House, the home of Duncan

Campbell, the brother of the man he had just murdered and whose body was now well downstream in Clan Campbell country. In all innocence, Duncan Campbell admitted Stewart into the house and offered him his hospitality.

That same night Campbell woke up to find the bloodstained figure of his brother Donald, standing at the foot of the bed. The spectre spoke to him saying: 'You are sheltering my murderer. I insist on my revenge.'

Campbell however, could not bring himself to violate the time-honoured code of hospitality, and for the next three nights his brother's ghost stood at his bedside. Before vanishing for the last time, the spectre raised its hand and said with reproach: 'Meet me at Ticonderoga.'

Duncan had never heard of Ticonderoga and could not make any sense of the spectre's message. But soon after Stewart left Inverawe House in safety, Campbell himself left to join his regiment, the Black Watch, and was sent out to America. There, the regiment was posted to a place which stood between New York State and Vermont, and here there was a fort occupied by the French – Fort Ticonderoga.

On 17 July 1758, the Black Watch attacked the fort and Duncan Campbell of Inverawe kept the appointment made by the sinister figure at the foot of his bed. It is here that legend and fact become confused. According to one source, that same night a young boy woke up at Inverawe House and cried out in terror at the sight of a tall Highlander bending over his bed. When he told his parents, they deduced that it had been the ghost of Duncan Campbell, come to tell of his death in America.

However, other sources tell us that Duncan Campbell died in Glasgow in 1760, as a result of injuries received in the battle for Fort Ticonderoga. Whichever way it was, the battle is commemorated in the name of the haunted bedroom. It is said that the ghost of Duncan Campbell is not yet at rest, and that it can often be seen in the form of a tall handsome figure in the Highland uniform of the eighteenth century, silently pacing the interior of the now derelict house.

A few years ago, an Aberdeen businessman, and his wife and dog, were stranded when his car broke down late one autumn evening in a dreary West Highland glen, far from a railway station and the nearest inhabited dwelling. He managed to run his car off the narrow road, out of harm's way, and got out to investigate his surroundings.

He found, about a quarter of a mile away, a narrow path which led down to the side of a loch, on the shore of which he could see a partly ruined manor house. At least it afforded some protection for the night and so, collecting his wife and his dog, he set off with them towards the old house. After making their way across a windswept moor and past a disused old churchyard, the path suddenly dipped down to the water's edge where at last they reached the house.

By now it had grown dark and they cautiously approached the house guided by the beam of a torch. The steps, which were dangerously worn, led into what had once been the main hall. There were thick overhead beams which looked as if they had supported what had been the heavily timbered floor of a large room on the right of the top of the staircase. Around the great hall ran a gallery, partly dismantled, which cast heavy shadows on the floor beneath. It was all very creepy and the last place on earth either of them would have chosen to spend the night, if given any choice.

After eating a bag of crisps and the remains of a bar of chocolate which had been bought earlier in the day, the couple decided to try and get what sleep they could in their unpleasant and uncomfortable surroundings. Finding the least uncomfortable places to settle down – the man and his dog in a corner of the gallery facing a bricked-up fireplace and his wife in a draught-free corner in the great hall just beneath him – they tried to get some sleep.

An angry growl from the dog and the screech of an owl suddenly awakened the couple. The husband could see by the luminous dial of his wristwatch that it was a little after one o'clock in the morning. Suddenly, he heard the creaking of loose floorboards, and by the light of the moon he could just discern a figure crouching by the bricked-up fireplace. He called out: 'Who's there?' but his shout was only answered by a terrified scream from his wife.

The dim figure seemed to resolve itself into that of a tall, well-built woman wearing a blue gown who seemed to be trying to dislodge some of the brickwork of the old fireplace. Then suddenly, she disappeared as if into thin air and his terrified wife's voice called out again. A deadly stillness had now come over the ruined old house and a cold draught seemed to blow through it. The woman in the blue gown had completely disappeared and the man was left staring at nothing but the bricked-up fireplace. She appeared to be so solid that he didn't realize she was anything other than a normal human being. But she had not passed him and there was no recess on this side of the hall where she could have hidden. She had simply vanished.

His wife told him that she had seen a woman in a blue gown stealing silently along the gallery, down the old staircase and over to the bricked-up fireplace, where she had then clutched feverishly at the bricks. When she cried out, the figure suddenly vanished.

The following day, the couple managed to walk to the nearest village and, while a mechanic went out to repair the car, they lunched at the village pub. Here they described their adventures to the landlord, who told them that they had spent the night in a reputedly haunted house, which once belonged to an old laird who had been married to a much younger and very beautiful wife. The woman was said to have been in love with a young local Casanova whom she used to meet in secret.

Their secret meetings went on for some time, until one night the laird returned home unexpectedly to find his wife in the arms of her lover in the grounds of the house. Unknown to them, he hid himself in the bushes and watched what went on. Noise and bustle in the courtyard, however, warned the lovers that the laird's men had returned, and the lady gave her lover whispered instructions as to where he should hide for the time being.

The young wife was wearing a blue gown and, later on, when she joined her husband in the great hall, he ironically complimented her on donning such a beautiful dress in honour of his return. Then he ordered her to dine with him. In the meantime, unknown to his wife, the laird's men had been dispatched to search the house and grounds and try to discover the whereabouts of the lover. They were unsuccessful, however.

As it was a cold night, the laird called out for a fire to be lit. His wife cried out that this was quite unnecessary and a waste of fuel; but her apprehensive glances towards the fireplace were not lost on her husband and told him all he needed to know about her lover's hiding place. He gave orders that the fireplace be immediately blocked up and while he held his screaming wife, the fireplace was bricked up before her eyes.

During the night, the frantic young woman came down and tried to pull out the bricks that now imprisoned her lover who had concealed himself in the wide chimney, but by that time the mortar had hardened and he was trapped to await a lingering death from thirst and hunger in his bricked-up prison. She tried for several nights to release him but without success. It is said that she pined away and died very soon afterwards.

Today, according to local tradition, the unhappy ghost of the Lady in Blue haunts the tomb of her lover, clutching at the brickwork in a vain attempt to free him. Ironically, the lover is thought to have escaped by climbing up the chimney and making his way across the rooftops to safety!

# 4   Hauntings Ecclesiastic

Melrose stands on the A6091, four miles to the south-east of Galashiels, right in the heart of romantic Scott country. This little town boasts one of the most outstanding ancient religious buildings in the whole of Scotland – Melrose Abbey; a memorial to the brotherhood between the Scots and the English and to the senseless destruction of the zealots of the Reformation.

The Abbey began life in the twelfth century, when a number of English masons were invited to Scotland by King David I to help build a monastery in the town. It was occupied by Cistercian monks who came from Rievaulx Abbey in North Yorkshire. Destroyed by King Edward II of England, it was rebuilt from a grant made for the purpose by Robert the Bruce, despite the hindrances caused by a number of attacks by Richard II. From about 1545 it was subjected to the tender mercies of Reformers, Covenanters and the local population, who regarded it as a convenient quarry whenever building stone was required, until virtually none of the work Robert the Bruce supervised was left standing.

The heart of Bruce is believed to lie in the vicinity of the High Altar, and a few yards away lie the remains of King Alexander II. His wife, Joanna, is buried here too, as are the remains of Michael Scott, whose tomb lies at the entrance to the sanctuary. The feeling of cold air, and a sense of unease sometimes felt on the south side of the Chancel, are said to be due to the psychic influences of Scott himself. Michael Scott was a witch, thought to have been born in the north-eastern border country. His claims to fame as a wizard are many, but today's scholars regard him as the leading intellectual in Europe in the first half of the thirteenth century.

He was reputed to have been able to command the sea by the help of demons. 'Mounted on the Devil's horse, he was bidden to ride towards the land, but on no account must he look back', wrote Edmund Sandford in 1675. However, terrified by the hideous noise of many waters behind him, Scott turned in his saddle and 'there the sea stopped, about eight miles from Carlisle'.

Scott is thought to have retired in old age to the Cistercian Abbey of Holm Cultram and to have died there about 1290, but it was at Melrose that he was buried and his tomb is in the vicinity of the abnormal sensations experienced by many of those affected by psychic influences.

However, perhaps the best-known ghost recorded at Melrose Abbey is that of a monk, a man who is said to have broken his vows and pursued a life of crime and vice, including vampirism. His ghost, often seen slithering along the ground in a prone position, haunts the area between the cloister garth and the chapter house to the east of the ruins.

The Gaelic name of Iona – I Chaluim Chille – literally means 'the island of the cell of Columba'. It was from Iona that, from AD 563 to AD 597, St Columba set out to spread the message of Christianity over much of heathen Scotland. Later, the island became famous as the burial place of the kings and princes of Scotland, as well as several Norwegian kings, who were influenced in their choice not only by its supposed sanctity, but also by a desire of preserving their remains from a fate awaiting those buried in less favoured spots.

The Norsemen frequently desecrated Iona, and the monastery erected by St Columba was repeatedly destroyed and restored again. Their longships sailed in, pillaging, burning and killing over and over again. It is these same Norse warriors that are condemned to relive their brutal attacks on the monks and villagers for all eternity.

Today, when the moon is unhidden by clouds, their ghostly longships are said to be seen gliding silently across the water with their crews scrambling up the vertical cliffs to the top of Tor Abb. Often, the sound of ghostly chanting can be heard coming from the restored monastic buildings, despite the onset of a ghostly invasion. Sir Walter Scott wrote that the invasion has occasionally been re-enacted in broad daylight and one sighting, during an air-raid alert in the autumn of 1941, is recorded as having set off an invasion scare in the operations room of RAF Fighter Command at Raigmore, Inverness!

After Iona had been repeatedly sacked, round about AD 900, St Andrews in Fife became the ecclesiastical capital of the Picts and a Columban church was founded here. By the twelfth century it had grown into a massive cathedral, only to be left in ruins following the Reformation. One part of this huge site is taken up by the ruined church and tower of St Rule, which dates from about 1127. Not much of the actual church remains today, except for its 110-foot tower.

There is a story told here of a visitor who, in the 1950s, walked up the narrow winding stairs of the tower, to see the wonderful panoramic view of the surrounding countryside, which this fine vantage point offers. He was about halfway up the dark winding staircase when he slipped on one of the worn stone steps and had to quickly grab the handrail to stop himself from falling. A little light penetrated a slit, and the visitor became aware of someone standing above him on the stairway. The figure wore a dark cassock with a girdle around the waist and, in a polite voice, asked: 'Are you all right? If you wish, you can take hold of my arm!

The figure was so solid and lifelike, the visitor said to him: 'No, I can manage, thank you,' at which the figure moved to one side to let him pass, so that within a half minute or so, he emerged at the top of the tower. Then it suddenly struck him; he had had to squeeze past the figure on the narrow winding steps, yet he never felt anything.

On returning to the ground, the visitor asked the custodian if anyone had come out of the entrance, and the answer he received convinced him that he had not only seen, but had also spoken to, the ghostly monk of St Rule's.

The story behind this particular haunting, is that some 250 years or more ago, the monk had been murdered in the tower by a jealous rival. Although his appearances are usually limited to the period just before and just after a full moon, the ghostly monk is always pleasant and friendly, and his manner is said to be most helpful no matter what time of day or night one might come across him!

Following the German occupation of Norway in April, 1940, and until the end of the Second World War, the town of Dumfries was the headquarters of the Free Norwegian Forces, and there are two separate and well-documented accounts of Norwegian servicemen encountering two of the ghosts which haunt the area between Castle Street and the river.

On the first occasion, one serviceman when returning to his billet on a late summer evening, stared in horror as a headless horseman appeared to gallop straight across the road a few yards in front of him and dissolve into one of the buildings. The terrified man was not aware of it, but he had just witnessed the ghost of a young man called MacMilligan who, several centuries ago, went courting a local girl but, on being challenged by her well-built brothers, decided that discretion was the better part of valour and rode off again. In the darkness, the young MacMilligan rode straight into an overhanging branch and his head was struck from his shoulders. The head then rolled back along the road and came to rest at the gates of Dumfries Priory.

Since that time, MacMilligan's headless ghost has been seen on a number of occasions, riding his horse, presumably in search of his head.

A different sighting took place in the same area in 1944, when two Norwegian servicemen were walking down Castle Street late one night. They clearly saw two figures rushing, as if away from a recently committed crime, towards the River Nith. At first it appeared as if one was chasing after the other. It was only later, when the men were discussing the incident, they realized that, although it was a still, frosty and moonlit night, they had not heard a sound, either of running footsteps or voices, from the two male figures who were running so energetically.

Although the two men (and the man who had witnessed the headless horseman) were unaware of it, all these activities had taken place on the site of what had been Dumfries Priory, near where the phantom horseman had disappeared. The sighting by the second two men can be backed up by historical fact.

It was in the Priory Church – the site of which is today marked by a tablet on one of the buildings – that in 1306, Robert the Bruce stabbed the Red Comyn during a violent quarrel. Not certain that he had killed the man, Bruce sent his retainer, Roger Kirkpatrick, back into the church to finish him off. Both men then hurried from the scene of their sacrilegious act – their resultant flight being witnessed by two Norwegian servicemen, who knew nothing of the town or its history, some 600 years later.

Bedlay Castle, at the junction of the A80 and the A757 at Chryston, about seven miles to the north-east of Glasgow, was built in the twelfth century as the official residence of the Bishops of Glasgow. However, in about 1350, a new manor and chapel were built, following the death, in rather suspicious circumstances, of Bishop Cameron who was found floating face downwards in a lake that existed there at the time.

This is a fine old castle and a ghost-hunter's paradise, with its fine collection of antiques, its bats and not forgetting the ghost of bishop Cameron. During the 1970s, it was occupied by an antique dealer and his family and very soon after their arrival there, the children complained of seeing the ghost of 'a big man'. His wife also complained of an invisible person who kept touching her hair. On other occasions, mysterious footsteps were heard walking along passageways or pacing backwards and forwards across empty rooms.

The castle was abandoned by the Church as far back as the late fourteenth century, but Bishop Cameron's ghost refused to go with the furnishings, preferring to remain on at Bedlay. In 1882, when Hugh McDonald published his *Rambles Around Glasgow*, he gave a very good account of the hauntings at Bedlay. At that time, the hauntings had become so bad and were the cause of so much distress, a local priest had to be called in to exorcise the place. However, he doesn't appear to have had a great deal of success, although the years have had the effect of softening the old bishop, as my information is that he is hardly, if ever, seen these days, except that on the odd occasion he can still be heard pounding the floorboards.

Isolated graveyards often have a ghostly reputation and there is a rather grim legend attached to the graveyard of Fearn Church, which stands on the B9166, about thirteen miles north-east of Invergordon.

Many years ago, a local farmer, on the very evening of his wife's burial, went to the house of a buxom girl who lived next to the church and asked her to marry him. As he was known to be a man of means, the girl quickly accepted his proposal and by nightfall, neither the girl nor the widower having wasted much time, they were both in bed together and making love. Suddenly the girl's mother returned home and was shocked to find her daughter naked in bed with a man whose wife was not yet cold in her grave, as she lost no time in reminding him.

The farmer laughed at her. 'She may look warm enough in her coffin,' he said, 'but she was cold enough when she was put there.'

Hardly had he spoken when his face became convulsed with terror because standing in the adjoining churchyard at Fearn, and peering at him through the window, was the shrouded figure of his dead wife. The terrified farmer quickly dressed and fled home, where he took to his bed at once and within a fortnight, died of a massive stroke.

As Lindisfarne, or Holy Island, is well to the north of Hadrian's Wall and so close to the Scottish mainland, I hope I can be excused for including it here, for it well deserves a mention. It stands just ten miles from Berwick-upon-Tweed and is reached by a causeway across the sands from Beal, just off the A1.

Lindisfarne Castle, the Priory and all the surrounding area from the mainland to the small island are steeped in ancient history. The beach is where the Vikings landed in 793 and many relics of their invasion have been discovered hereabouts. The castle, now owned by the National Trust, was built in 1550 to protect Holy Island Harbour from attack. It was restored and converted into a private house by Sir Edwin Lutyens in 1903.

The monastery was founded in the seventh century, but it was later destroyed by the Norsemen led by such terrifyingly named warriors as Ivor the Boneless and Erick Bloodaxe. Following the Norman Conquest of 1066, the early monastery was re-erected as a priory. The present ruins are evidence of Henry VIII's Dissolution of the Monasteries and the castle was built of stones taken from there.

If one stands on the ancient rocks near the priory ruins, particularly on a bleak, grey day, with the ever-present wind tugging at one's clothing, it is not difficult to visualize the terrified monks, all those centuries ago, rushing across the beach with their relics and valuables, pursued by the bearded Vikings, their battle-axes swinging, swords flashing and their cries of victory following the decapitation of a fleeing monk. In fact, the monks put up a valiant fight for their treasure, and much of it was saved, but at the cost of many of their lives.

It is thought to be one of the victims of the Viking invasion who is seen periodically drifting quickly across the causeway to the security of Beal. Those who have seen him often admit to having no previous knowledge of the history of the area and are usually surprised to learn that the apparition of the grey-clad figure they have clearly seen, often in great detail, could in fact be that of a man who was killed whilst trying to protect the priory treasures over a thousand years ago. It is only after he has faded into the sand that realization may suddenly dawn upon them.

At the turn of the century, there stood an old church on an isolated road near Biggar, some twenty miles to the west of Peebles.

One day a stranger to the district was walking along the lonely road leading to the town, when he found himself caught in a sudden storm. Seeing the church ahead of him, he ran to it to shelter and was relieved to discover that the door was unlocked. Going inside, he was surprised to find a service in progress, so he quietly seated himself on a pew at the back until the storm had eased. He had not been sitting there long when another man entered the building and walked up the centre aisle. To his horror, the stranger saw that the man was headless!

But the worst was yet to come. Leaning against a pillar and looking at the vicar with an expression of amusement on his face, was a tall, dark, sinister man. When the vicar had finished his sermon and was about to descend from the pulpit, he caught sight of the dark man and his face suddenly contorted with terror.

Weird, ghostly music then filled the church, accompanied by loud, mocking laughter and the whole building seemed now to be lit up with some unearthly light. Then, suddenly, and much to the astonishment of the traveller – everything vanished, figures, vicar, music, light, everything in fact, and the whole place was plunged into total darkness.

As soon as he had recovered from his terror, which had rooted him to the spot, the poor traveller groped his way out of the church and, disregarding the heavy downpour, ran as fast as his legs would carry him to Biggar. There he told his story and was even more surprised to discover that the old church had long since been abandoned, and was well known to be haunted. There is nothing in the local records to explain the haunting, but there is still a whispered story circulating in the area, which suggests that one rector, who had been the incumbent many years ago, had been defrocked when it was discovered he had been involved for many years in black magic practices in the church late at night.

Some years ago, a seaman was seen on several evenings walking in the vicinity of the churchyard at Kenovay on the Island of Tiree. This being a small, close-knit community, his presence caused considerable interest, although with typical Scots reserve, no one appears to have spoken to him or asked him who he was or why he was there.

Several months later, a body was washed up on the beach at Hynish Bay, dressed in the same clothes the figure wore when he was seen strolling in and around Kenovay churchyard. Most locals suggested that the man had been drowned after falling into the sea, but the local fishermen, who knew the water around Tiree better than most, insisted that the currents around Hynish Bay made it impossible for the body to have come from anywhere but out at sea. Although it was badly mutilated by being pounded on the rocks, the body was not in any way decomposed as it should have been after long immersion in the water.

Eventually the unfortunate seaman was buried in Kenovay churchyard and it is there that his ghost can often be sighted, drifting quietly amongst the tombstones. No one knows to this day who he was or where he came from.

Adjoining the church at Dalarossie in the Findhorn Valley, south-west of Forres, there is a glebe of land which has a rather strange story attached to it.

Many years ago, a team of men from Strathnairn challenged an equal number of men from Strathdurn to a game of shinty – a Scottish ball game not unlike hockey. The match was fixed up to take place on Christmas Day which that year fell on a Sunday. The Straithnairn men turned up at the appointed time, but their opponents did not, so they picked sides from amongst themselves and proceeded with their game on the Sabbath.

It is said that within a year, all the players in this unhallowed game were dead and were buried in the level part of the churchyard, next to the river. Ever since that time, whenever Christmas Day falls on a Sunday, a phantom team can be seen repeating their game of shinty on the glebe at dead of night.

My maternal grandmother was born in the late 1870s and, like most girls from large poor Victorian families, when she was old enough she was sent into service. She was employed as a maid at the old manse in Kirkmichael, on the B7045 a few miles north-west of Straiton, and on two separate occasions she had rather frightening experiences there.

On the first occasion, in the early hours of the morning, she saw the figure of an old man dressed in a white flowing robe. On his head he wore a garland of leaves, and he appeared to be holding in his hands a sickle which glinted as if it was made of gold. Later, when she was alone in the house, she was terrified when a sudden cry of anguish came from nowhere to rise to a crescendo before dying away again.

Apparently she told the master of the house, a Presbyterian preacher, who dismissed the first incident as the effects of the early morning mist on the mind of a silly young Sassenach girl, who was only half awake at the best of times. The origin of the cry, he said, must have come from a barn owl trapped in one of the chimneys.

What he knew, but failed to tell her, was that the old manse was thought to have been built on the site of an ancient Druid place of worship – and human sacrifice was a major part of their religion.

Some years ago, the old manse at Durness, which stands on the A838 on the north-western tip of Scotland, was occupied by a minister who, on account of the strange knocks heard each night on his front door and believing them to be supernatural in origin, asked his friend, the minister at Kinlochbervie, to go and see him, although he was careful not to reveal why he had sent for him.

The minister rode on horseback the twenty miles or so to Durness on Christmas Eve and, not knowing why his friend had sent for him, he tethered his horse in the stable before going into the vicarage where he was warmly received by his ecclesiastical colleague. After an excellent dinner and some friendly conversation, the two men retired to the study, the minister still unaware of his reason for being there. Then suddenly, the mysterious knocks began on the front door and making some excuse, the Durness minister asked his friend from Kinlochber-vie to go to the door and see who was there. The visitor innocently opened the door, not knowing who or what he would meet, and to his horror, he saw standing on the doorstep, the ghostly figure of a man swathed in a shroud.

Returning to the study some moments later, his face a deathly white, he rebuked the Durness minister for not giving him warning of the haunting, because he could have come prepared to deal with the situation. In fact he was so angry, he stormed out of the house, saddled his horse and, despite the fact it was well after midnight, rode the twenty miles back to his own manse at Kinlochbervie.

By the new year he had become seriously ill and by the end of January he died at the comparatively early age of 46. Then within weeks his wife, who was a few years younger, suddenly joined him, after collapsing outside Kinlochbervie Church. So far no rational explanation has been put forward to suggest the reason behind the haunting at Durness Manse, or for the mysterious deaths which so quickly followed it.

There is an interesting and amusing legend concerning the monks of Dryburgh Abbey, which stands alongside the B6356, a few miles to the south east of Melrose.

Most of the monks of Dryburgh kept their vows of poverty, chastity and obedience, although of the three, the least popular was the vow of poverty. But those who broke this vow – and by all accounts many of them did – pleaded that they were not doing so for their own self-interest or in the spirit of rebellion. (When that was the case, they were not above breaking the other two vows.) No, they argued that they had the welfare of the abbey community at heart. What was the sense in being poor, when there was plenty of wealth to be had without harming anyone, or depriving anyone of their rights? There were benefactors and well-wishers who only needed to be 'encouraged' to leave their lands and money to the abbey, with no loss to themselves. After all, would it not benefit their souls when they passed through into that great beyond? They would have prayers in plenty to help speed them on their way.

One old laird of Meldrum was a devoutly religious man who had led an impeccable life, and was a friend and benefactor to the abbey. He was a kindly man who had never married, so he had no son to inherit his estate, nor any near relations. If he were to leave all his lands and money to the abbey, the community would benefit and no one would suffer, and he had been encouraged by the monks to do just this.

When they heard that he was seriously ill and on the point of death, the Prior and his bursar went to visit the old laird and give him spiritual comfort. But they were too late: when they arrived the old laird was already dead. They prayed for his soul and then looked for his last will and testament, but there was nothing to be found, not even a scrap of paper. This was a disaster. Now, some distant kinsman would probably turn up and claim the estate, and there would be nothing to prove the laird's intention of leaving everything to Dryburgh Abbey.

Then the bursar had a bright idea which met with the Prior's immediate approval. They rushed back to Dryburgh Abbey and told the Father Abbot and the brethren of their plan, and everyone commended the bursar for his clever thinking. The plan was that they would conceal the laird's death, remove his body and replace it with a certain poor man called Thomas Dickson, who lived in the neighbourhood and who bore a remarkable resemblance to the late laird.

Thomas Dickson was approached with the idea. For a goodly fee, he was to act as if he was on the point of death and as an added bonus, he would benefit from the monks' prayers both here and in the hereafter, providing, of course, that he kept the whole matter secret.

This being agreed, the body of the laird was carried with due reverence into another room and Thomas took his place in the bed. The bursar brought a lawyer and two of his apprentice clerks from Melrose, and he and the Prior sat silently by the bedside with the men of law. Thomas contrived to look as if he was dying and to speak in a weak and feeble voice. He declared himself to be of sound mind and clear intention and to be able to make his signature. Then he dictated his 'will':

'Hear me, reverend father, and you my good man of law. I hereby bequeath to that honest man Thomas Dickson, this house and all its plenishing, my lands and estate of Meldrum, my moneys and possessions, having long known him as a most honourable man who has suffered much poverty and hardship!'

He added a few legacies – mere tokens – to the monks, then he signed the laird's name in a shaking hand, groaned and sank back in the bed with his eyes closed. The lawyer took it all down, and his clerks signed as witness that all was in order. The two monks, nearer to death with shock and rage than Thomas was at this time, could do nothing; they were caught in a web of their own weaving.

To denounce Thomas would be to give themselves and the community away and bring the law down on their heads. Thomas would, of course, be punished for his fraudulent act and deprived of the legacy which he had made to himself, but that would be nothing at all compared to the scandal that would fall on the Abbey.

What passed between the monks and Thomas after the lawyer departed will never be known. The old laird was buried with due rites. Mass was said for the peace of his soul, and Thomas even requested that he should pay for another. The will was never disputed, Thomas took possession and lived for many years in comfort, being careful to pay the monks their legacy.

Today, we are told that on the anniversary of the old laird's death, the ghosts of Thomas Dickson and the monks of Dryburgh Abbey, can still be seen and heard, saying Mass for the soul of his benefactor.

There is a grim little legend surrounding the old churchyard which stands beside the ruined church on St Mungo's Island, at the entrance to Loch Leven. According to local legend, this old church was built by the Camerons of Lochiel many centuries ago, as a penance for some minor offence or other. During the 1750s, when the church and churchyard were still in use, it was said to have been the scene of a rather bizarre supernatural occurrence.

A local farmer had been buried and for several nights following his funeral, the whole neighbourhood was kept awake by his ghostly voice, which called on a certain village man to come and help him. After suffering the noise for almost a week, the locals pleaded with the man to do as the ghostly voice bid and visit the graveyard at the dead of night.

The villager was persuaded, rather reluctantly, and went to the graveyard late at night, where he was astonished to find the head and shoulders of the dead man sticking up out of the grave. Terrified, he asked the corpse what it wanted and why it had disturbed the neighbourhood in such a fashion. The dead man is said to have told him that in his younger days, he had sworn a solemn oath that he would marry a certain woman and he would never forsake her, so long as his head remained on his shoulders. Therefore, the man must cut his head from his body!

Taking pity on the dead man's predicament, the villager picked up a scythe which lay nearby and severed the head from the corpse, close to the ground, with one stroke. At this, relieved of his burden, the dead man lowered the trunk of his body back down into the grave, abandoning his severed head and, so far as anyone knows, his headless corpse now rests in peace.

A similar and rather sinister story, concerns the church at Fincharn, on the B840 at the southern end of Loch Awe.

Here, there once lived a tailor, a very sceptical man, who absolutely refused to believe in the existence of ghosts. One night, following an argument at the village inn, during which time the tailor defied anyone to prove the existence of ghosts, he was bet that despite his disbelief, he wouldn't dare spend the rest of the night alone, in the village churchyard and bring back the skull which lay on the window of the old church as a constant reminder that man cannot escape death.

The tailor, having drunk quite a lot of whisky, expressed disdain at so slight a task and said he would do better than that. He bet a guinea that on the following night, he would not only stay inside the church itself with the skull for company, but he would also make a pair of trousers before the cock crowed. The bet was agreed and, the following night, the tailor took his place in the empty church, selecting as his makeshift workbench a flat gravestone resting on four low pillars and, with a lighted candle at his side, he began the task of making a pair of trousers.

For the first hour he quietly sewed away, keeping his spirits up in such a gloomy place by whistling and singing all the songs and reels he knew. Midnight came and went but, other than the occasional fluttering of bats, nothing disturbed his peace. Just before one o'clock in the morning, however, he heard a noise coming from a gravestone near the church door and, looking round, he thought he saw the heavy gravestone moving. He put it down to his imagination, convinced that this was an illusion caused by the flickering candle. So he shrugged his shoulders and went back to his work.

Moments later, his hair stood on end as a hollow voice from under the gravestone said: 'See the great mouldering hand, tailor!' Sure enough, a skeletal hand appeared out of the tomb.

But the tailor mustered his courage and resumed his sewing and singing. A little later, the same unearthly voice called out, louder than before: 'See the great mouldering skull, tailor!' The tailor ignored it and carried on sewing, although he sewed a little faster now, his hands shaking, and when he tried to whistle through his dry lips, he found he couldn't.

Then the voice, sounding more ominous and reverberating around the empty church, cried out: 'See the great mouldering shoulders, tailor!' Now frightened, the tailor sewed still faster, lengthening the span of his stitches as gradually more and more of the corpse emerged from the grave, the dead man's haunch and finally, his foot appearing.

At this, the tailor knew it was time to be off. He hastily completed the last few stitches, knotted the thread and broke it off with his teeth. Then, snatching up the completed trousers and blowing out the candle, he made a dash for the door. The corpse pursued him and, as the tailor ran out across the threshold, it aimed a blow at him. Fortunately it missed, but for years afterwards, the grisly imprint of its hand and fingers could be seen on the door post.

Then, just as it seemed the corpse would catch up with him, the cocks began to crow. It was dawn and the dead man, like the vampire it surely was, had to return to the tomb. As for the tailor, he returned to the inn triumphantly bearing the trousers and he won his bet. He no longer disbelieved in the supernatural – but when he told his friends what had taken place in the church that night, no one would believe *him*! There must be a moral here somewhere.

A gravestone in Hobkirk churchyard, on the A6088 about eight miles south-east of Hawick, marks the burial place of the eighteenth-century minister, the Revd Nicol Edgar, who is said to have laid to rest a particularly troublesome ghost which haunted the church.

It appears that this public-spirited action gained the minister an uncanny reputation, for after his death it was thought that his ghost might wander from its grave in the churchyard. So, it was decided that he should be reburied outside the village. Whilst the corpse was being carried across the moor, the bearers slipped and the ice-cold hand of the dead minister struck one of them. The poor fellow fled in panic.

The body remained where it was until the next day, when it was carefully returned to its original resting place, and where the gravestone can still be found today.

The Revd Thomas Mackay was the minister at Lairg, on the A836 in Sutherland. He was a rather lovable eccentric who always wore the full clerical dress of a bishop during his lifetime and he died peacefully in his sleep in 1803, mourned by all who knew and loved him.

One fine sunny day in the summer of 1827, the two daughters of the incumbent were sitting in the dining-room of the old manse at Lairg when they heard footsteps approaching the dining-room door. The door quietly opened and they saw, standing just inside the doorway, a very old thin man, dressed entirely in black, with knee breeches and buckles, black stockings and buckled shoes. He glanced casually round the room before walking away again, leaving the door open behind him.

One of the girls ran upstairs to tell her father that a very old bishop had come in and was looking for him. The minister hurried downstairs to greet the visitor – but he had vanished completely. The manse stood in its own extensive grounds and everything could be seen for well over a quarter of a mile all around, yet there was no trace of the old man anywhere. Later, when the girls described him to the older members of the congregation, they were told that their description matched that of the late Revd Mackay.

Today the old manse is no more, but locals say that the ghost of the old minister still haunts the site on occasion. Not so many years ago, two poachers who were on the site late at night became so terrified, on account of the unearthly sounds coming from the direction of the ruined manse, that they abandoned their gear and fled in terror to the nearest public bar!

# 5   Haunted Highways and Byways

It was Hogmanay, 1921, and John McDonald had been entertaining with his melodion at a concert at the old school in Dunphail, which was situated beside the old Highland Railway line, a mile or so from the former Dunphail railway station. Knowing full well that at this time of night the last train had long since left Dunphail station, John was making his way home taking the quick route by walking alongside the railway track.

It was just a little after midnight on a beautiful crisp, moonlit night and although it was New Year's Eve and he had enjoyed himself, John was quite sober, whistling as he strode along without a care in the world. He reached the junction with the main Perth line which curved away to the south, when suddenly a strange feeling of fear came over him.

The hair began to rise on the back of his neck and he had the horrible feeling that there was a train approaching him from behind. He turned and looked back along the line and, sure enough, to his horror, he saw a train bearing down on him round a slight curve in the line. Clouds of smoke poured from the chimney of the engine and he could see four brightly lit carriages, although there were no passengers aboard. Worse still, it was obvious from the glow of the fire which clearly lit up the cab, showing the controls in sharp relief, that there was neither a driver nor a fireman on the footplate.

As John was quickly scrambling up the embankment to get away from the speeding train, he noticed something else – something which sent ice-cold shivers of fear down his spine. The train was not making contact with the track, but appeared to be some two feet or so above the rails, as if it was floating! Petrified with fear, he sat on the embankment and watched as the ghostly train floated past him and out of sight in a swirl of mist.

Other people have experienced the ghostly train, even in recent years, though the track has long been lifted. Today, there is hardly any visible sign that the railway has ever been here, except for the ghostly train which still rushes past from time to time. Not many years ago, a young woman was walking along the old track bed one evening, not far from the site of Dunphail station, when she had a strange feeling that something was about to happen. Suddenly, some unknown force hit her in the back, hurling her to the ground. For some time she was unable to get up and when she did finally struggle to her knees, she crawled home in a very bad way.

One night early in the 1960s, two men travelling in a car, along the A75 between Dumfries and Annan, had what must surely qualify as the most terrifying experience of the century. They had been touring the borders in a small car and were on their way home after stopping off at Dumfries for a snack and some petrol. Just before midnight they found themselves on the A75 with some twelve miles or so to go before reaching Annan. It was a dry moonlit night and the road stretched empty for several miles ahead of them.

Suddenly, the car headlights picked up the figure of an old woman rushing towards them and waving her arms wildly. Before the driver had time to react, the figure simply vanished into thin air. But worse was to come, for the old woman then seemed to be followed by an endless stream of figures that loomed out of nowhere; cats, dogs, farm animals and an old man with his long hair flying who seemed to be screaming, yet no noise came from his gaping mouth.

The driver kept swerving from side to side in an effort to miss hitting the strange figures, until he suddenly realized that they made no actual contact with the car. He therefore began to think it was his imagination. However, a quick glance at his passenger, sitting terrified and wild-eyed beside him, told him that this was no imagination, he was seeing the terrifying phantoms too.

As they continued to drive through the mass of open-mouthed and wild-looking creatures, there was a sudden drop in the temperature inside the vehicle and the driver felt as if some force was trying to gain control of the car by wrestling the steering-wheel from him. Then both men began to feel suffocated and on opening the window, bitterly cold air rushed in, along with a cacophony of screaming, high-pitched laughter and cackling noises which seemed to be mocking the terrified occupants.

Unable to control the car any longer, the driver pulled in at the side of the road at which point they were immediately attacked by an invisible and violent force which bombarded the car, rocking it from side to side until the two men began to feel sick. They both opened the doors and leapt out into the road – and immediately all was quiet; the road and surrounding countryside was still and utterly deserted. Yet as soon as they got back into the vehicle and shut the doors, the shaking and bouncing began again, this time accompanied by unearthly laughter. Invisible fists seemed to strike the car from every single angle and a high wind seemed to suddenly spring up, adding to the terror.

Deciding that the only sensible thing to do was get away from the place as quickly as possible, the driver pushed the car into gear and drove off slowly through the weird figures, which continued to loom suddenly out of nowhere, and the terrifying noises which came from every direction. Often, the figures would stop in the path of the vehicle, as if daring the driver to run them down, but he drove a steady and straight course and, just as it seemed he would hit them, the strange figures evaporated.

After driving like this for about two miles, the two men suddenly saw ahead of them, the comforting red glow of a large furniture van's rear lights. The driver suddenly became aware that the van was stationary and he was approaching it too fast. Exhausted by the previous events, his reactions were too slow and he found to his horror that there was no time to take evasive action. He was surely going to collide with the rear of the stationary vehicle.

Shouting a warning to his passenger, the driver steeled himself for the inevitable crash as the furniture van loomed larger and larger – and then, just before the moment of impact, the furniture van suddenly disappeared!

Shattered, drained of strength and totally mystified, the two men continued on their way. Then they realized that the car had slowed to a crawl, the noises and high wind had died away and they were relieved to find themselves on the outskirts of Annan. The whole terrifying incident had lasted over thirty minutes.

It is difficult to discover what brought about the strange events of that night, or who the ghostly figures were. There are tales that years ago witchcraft was practised in the area, but whether there was any connection one cannot say. And what about the phantom furniture van – what story lies behind that I wonder?

The late Elliott O'Donnell was never a man to spend idle days by the fireside. He was a born adventurer, the pattern set in his youth when he would tramp over hill and dale in his native Ireland, like a knight-errant in search of dragons. It took him years to settle down to a career as a writer, after roaming the world as a ranch-hand, actor, journalist and schoolmaster. When he died in Somerset in May 1965, at the age of 93, he was acknowledged as Britain's greatest ghost-hunter, and writer on the supernatural.

O'Donnell was also a fine fly fisherman and one of his favourite stories concerned an incident which took place at the turn of the century, when he was fishing Noran Water near Tannadice in Angus.

It had been an unusually wet summer and with so much rain the river was swollen. Hoping to profit by the conditions and return with a basket full of trout, he set off early one evening with his rod. On arriving at the riverside he set to work at once, and had been fishing for about an hour without so much as a nibble at the bait, when he suddenly felt he was no longer alone. Looking around he could see no one, yet he still had the feeling that someone was standing over him, as he heard what he later described as 'a deep drawn sigh'.

Not once, but several times there seemed to be a slight swishing sound, as if some other angler was casting his line quite close by. On each of these occasions, O'Donnell was rather startled and looked around sharply. But no one was there, he had the whole swollen stretch of river and its banks, as far as he could see, all to himself.

Nevertheless, the feeling that someone was standing beside him didn't lessen. In fact, it grew even more pronounced and, in time, became so unbearable that he left the spot and moved to another some distance away. But it was no use. He had not been in the new position very long before the same thing happened. He became conscious, once more, of being watched, and again he heard the long-drawn-out sigh and occasional swishes.

After a few more minutes O'Donnell moved on yet again but,

when he next settled down to fish, the sounds began once more and, no matter how many fresh places he tried, it was the same. Finally, his nerves became so jangled that he decided to abandon fishing for the night. He had taken his rod to pieces and was about to pick up his empty basket, when an old farm-hand approached him and asked if he had caught much.

O'Donnell replied that he had not had so much as a bite, and the farmhand replied: 'And you're not likely to as long as you fish in such company!'

Surprised, O'Donnell asked him what he meant, and the farm-hand said scornfully: 'I mean your companion. That tall man in knickerbockers. He cleared off just as I came up. He may be a friend of yours, but you'd do well to leave him behind when you come here again. I watched you both from a distance, and he kept following you about and getting his line mixed up in yours. Him a fisherman. Why, with that long, lean body of his and that white face, he looked more like a ghost.'

As a boy, Elliott O'Donnell frequently stayed with an aunt in her large old mansion in Angus. The house was in a lovely part of the countryside, which the young O'Donnell loved to roam on his bicycle.

One evening while out riding he collided with a large boulder and although he was unhurt, his cycle suffered a badly buckled front wheel and he was obliged to leave it at the nearby railway station and walk back to his aunt's house. It was quite late in the evening when he began to walk the five miles back to the old mansion; a prospect which he didn't find altogether cheering.

He had covered about a quarter of the distance, walking with long swinging strides, when he suddenly heard footsteps behind him. They appeared to be those of a heavily built man, but there was something so peculiar about them that he instinctively looked round. By now it was quite dark, and the moon had not yet put in an appearance, so he could see nothing or no one. O'Donnell stopped and the strange footsteps also stopped. He walked on again and the footsteps began again, but they now began to be so erratic that he thought they could only belong to someone who was drunk.

On either side of the road there was nothing but open ground and in the darkness a feeling of loneliness and isolation overcame him, that he began to feel quite frightened. Determined to confront the drunken man and demand to know why he was following him in this strange manner, O'Donnell stopped again and turned round. As before, the darkness was so intense that he could see nothing clearly, but forcing himself to appear quite calm, he shouted out: 'Hello. You there! Who are you? What do you want?'

The footsteps ceased, but there was no reply. He called out again, louder and more forcibly, but the result was still the same. O'Donnell walked on again but the mysterious footsteps continued to follow him. He now began to panic slightly and set off at a run and, to his horror, the footsteps ran after him, sometimes closing in on him, then gradually falling behind again, until they sounded faint and far away. They continued in this way until he was almost in sight of the old mansion, when they abruptly stopped.

Knowing his aunt to be an upstanding God-fearing woman who was sceptical about anything connected with the supernatural, O'Donnell said nothing to her about his adventure when he arrived home. But he was determined to walk the same road again the following evening and see if the same thing happened.

The next night the weather was all that he could desire. The sky was cloudless and full of stars, and there was a glorious full moon. O'Donnell had walked about halfway to the railway station, and was by then beginning to think it had all been in his imagination, when suddenly in addition to the sound of his own footsteps, he heard the familiar eerie sound of others behind him. He swung round at once but, as before, there was no one to be seen. Yet the sounds continued. The footsteps came nearer and nearer with terrifying regularity.

Suddenly on the white surface of the road, almost exactly in the centre, he saw a black shadowy figure advancing with the footsteps and rapidly drawing close. Terrified, for there was something indescribably eerie about both the footsteps and the figure, O'Donnell stepped to one side to let it pass. As it went by he saw, with a freezing chill, that the figure was apparently that of a short, stout man – but he was headless. There was a well defined neck yet, beyond it, where the head should have been, there was nothing!

He stood paralysed for some time and, when he next became aware of his surroundings and glanced round, all was deathly quiet. There was no sign of the shadowy figure anywhere.

Many years after the death of his aunt, O'Donnell returned to the area and whilst he was there he made some enquiries in the neighbourhood, eventually coming across an aged farm-worker, who told him that as a boy, he had often heard his father talk of a headless ghost on that part of the road. It would appear that a great many years ago, an old tramp had been found murdered by the roadside, and it was generally thought to be his ghost which haunted the vicinity of the crime on certain nights of the year.

Early in 1746, Bonnie Prince Charlie and his advisers realized that their hope of defeating the army of King George and marching on London was futile. The English people had not risen to support the Young Pretender, as he had thought they would, and it was now apparent that the French were not sending an army to help. So, with certain defeat staring him in the face, Charles turned north and headed for the safety of the Highlands.

He was forced to fight a rearguard action all the way, his army dwindling all the time as members deserted, or dropped off as they passed through their home towns and villages. Thus, in early March, less than 5,000 half-starved and weary Jacobite soldiers crossed the mountains, and at dawn on 16 April 1746, they drew up in formation on Culloden Moor to face the well-disciplined force of 9,000 men under the command of the Duke of Cumberland, in a last desperate stand.

The Battle of Culloden was really not much more than a short and bloody clash. Outnumbered, the Highlanders were cut to pieces by accurate gunfire and, lacking ammunition themselves, they were finally reduced to throwing stones. They fought heroically, no one can deny that, but in the end they died where they stood. No quarter was given and no quarter was asked for on that terrible day. At the end of the battle, Bonnie Prince Charlie managed to escape overseas and the old Highland system of loyalty, and the bonding of son to father, clansman to lord, was swept away forever.

Since that day in 1746, the battlefield of Culloden has had a reputation for being disturbingly haunted, following the horror of hand-to-hand fighting and the cold-blooded butchery of even the seriously wounded. As with many battlefields, individual ghosts and whole fighting armies have been seen ever since.

Not long after the battle, the spectral figure of a tall young Highland soldier was seen near the site, with an expression of great sadness on his face. Witnesses claimed to have heard him mutter: 'Defeated. Defeated', before suddenly vanishing. Several claims of a ghostly army suddenly materializing have been made, as have claims of hearing cries of pain, gunfire and the clash of arms.

One day, in quite recent years, a man travelling on the Euston-Inverness train looked out of the carriage window as it skirted the battlefield. He claimed to have seen an enormous band of troops in the sky, milling around as if engaged in battle. He said the whole apparition was in full colour; the red of the English uniforms and the contrasting colours of the standards were easily identifiable. Some time afterwards, this same passenger saw the famous painting by Paul Sandby, which is notable for its authentic portrayal of the Battle of Culloden, and he said he recognized many of the banners and soldiers he had seen suspended in the sky above the distant mountains.

Other ghosts at Culloden – which is on the B9006, five miles east of Inverness – take on different forms. Sometimes prone bodies are seen in the ground, as if the earth has suddenly become transparent. There are vague local stories which tell of a troop of ghostly soldiers being led by an officer in a Hussar's uniform and mounted on a big grey horse. Over the years there have been numerous reported sightings of strange lights over the battlefields and many people visiting the monument, which stands on the site, have been overcome by the feeling of terror, which only fierce hand-to-hand fighting can generate.

Scotland's past warfare is the source of many apparitions. One such ghostly phenomenon can be found near Inverary Castle, on the borders of Loch Fyne, about 60 miles north-west of Glasgow. Inverary Castle is the home of the Dukes of Argyll and has been the headquarters of the Clan Campbell for nearly six hundred years. Beside the castle runs the A83, which links the A819 going north to Dalmally. It is on this road that a ghostly army has been reported several times, marching in formation and dressed in the red coats of Cumberland's troops. The men are said to be seen marching six abreast, with colours flying, and are followed by a motley group of women and children carrying cooking equipment.

South of Fort William, the A82 runs alongside Loch Leven and into Glen Coe which is the scene of one of the most gruesome and tragic massacres in the history of Scotland. The grim majesty of Glen Coe is a fitting backdrop to this tragedy. The massacre of February 1692, when forty members of the Clan McDonald were killed in the half-light of a winter's dawn by their guests, a company of Campbell militia, was by modern standards quite small. But it has given birth to some endearing legends. To this day the nine of diamonds is known as the Curse of Scotland because the pips on the card bear some resemblance to the arms of the Master of Stair who, next to William III, bore the greatest responsibility for the slaughter.

Tourists only see the glen in summer, but to see it in all its stark grandeur, with a weak sun breaking through the shifting clouds creating a scene of awesome beauty, and to feel the ghostly presence which haunts the jagged rocks, then one should visit it as I did, on a cold and windy March morning. A local farmer told me that the best time to visit the glen is on the anniversary of the massacre – February 13. If you go at daybreak and particularly if the weather is stormy in this valley of streams, you can feel for yourself the vengeful phantoms of the Clan McDonald. Perhaps you may also hear the phantom pipes which are said to have led the Campbell troops astray in the mountains, as they made their way back to Fort William. Or you may catch sight of the gaunt motionless figures of the ghosts of the McDonalds staring out at you from amongst the rocks.

As one local told me during my visit: 'This is one place of death where the dead will not rest in peace.' On such a day it was possible to believe him.

The historic streets of Edinburgh boast several ghosts, the best known being in the area around the beautiful Charlotte Square. Here the tourist will find four well-authenticated spectres: a phantom coach, a woman in eighteenth-century dress, a mournful-looking old beggar and the shadowy figure of a monk.

Perhaps not quite so well known are the eerie ghosts to be found south of the castle in the Old Town. Here in a hollow at the foot of the Castle Rock, is a large open space known as the Grassmarket; the traditional site of Edinburgh's gallows. The actual site of the gallows is identified by a plaque close to the West Bow. In this road there once lived two of Edinburgh's most notorious criminals, Major Weir and Lord Ruthven. Lord Ruthven's ghost was said to have appeared in the doorway of his former home but, when this was demolished, his shadowy figure was seen quite often, flitting through the area dressed as on the day of his execution.

Major Weir, a diabolical villain tainted by the evils of the black arts, has haunted this street ever since his execution over three hundred years ago. He established himself in a house in West Bow in the mid-seventeenth century. In 1649, he was appointed commander of the city guard and was in charge of the execution of the Royalist Marquis of Montrose. Weir's zeal in the Presbyterian cause was well known, and he was a much respected, if not much loved, Edinburgh figure. He never married, and for years shared his house with his elder sister, Grizel.

He was often seen roaming the streets of the city, the scourge of the wicked citizens of Edinburgh and the terror of the local Roman Catholics, dressed in a long black cloak and carrying a staff, reputed to have magical properties and which was said to be 'alive'. Legend says that his magical staff acted as his servant, going by itself on shopping errands, answering the Major's door to his visitors and clearing the way in front of its master when he went out into the streets.

Suddenly, at the age of 69, he confessed to leading citizens of the city that he was a servant of the Devil. His whole life, he said, had been polluted by unspeakable crimes and he had indulged in revolting practices, with his sister as his accomplice. At first it was thought that he was insane, but when doctors examined him they found he was of sound mind. Eventually, on Weir's own insistence, both he and his sister were arrested and brought to trial. It now seems clear that Grizel was demented and, despite the doctors' opinions, it seems that like the old Major she had been deeply disturbed by the hag-ridden beliefs of the times.

When they were arrested Grizel advised the guards to seize Weir's staff, telling them that it was a gift from the Devil and the source of her brother's power. At the trial of the unfortunate pair in 1670, neighbours recalled several strange occurrences which had taken place at Weir's house in West Bow. Major Weir confessed to having been visited in his room after dark by the Devil, and his sister confessed that both she and her brother took nightly rides in a phantom coach.

But their conviction rested mainly on their confessions to

necromancy, immorality, dealings with a familiar spirit, and Grizel's ability to spin abnormal quantities of yarn. They were both sentenced to be strangled and burnt. Major Weir's execution took place outside the city walls and his magic staff was burnt with him. A witness stated that the stick 'gave rare turnings and was long a-burning as also himself'. Grizel was hanged on a gibbet in the Grassmarket. When she was about to be executed she tried to remove her clothes, whereupon the executioner turned her prematurely off the ladder.

Following their execution, stories began to circulate about a huge woman who, laughing insanely, emerged from the ground outside the Major's former home. Sometimes the whole street was lit up by eerie lights carried by ghostly figures. Even today, the ghost of Major Weir is said to arrive at the scene on a headless horse and surrounded by flames. Many people still believe that Satan arrives shortly before dawn in a coach to take the Major and his spectral sister back, after giving them a few hours leave of absence from Hell to enjoy a spectral version of their earthly orgies!

But far more tangible and well recorded are the numerous sightings of Weir's ghostly sister, her face and hands said to be blackened and distorted by fire, and of Major Weir without a head. Many people claim to have heard the eerie sound of his staff as it tap-taps its way across the Grassmarket.

Towards the end of the seventeenth century, a shocking murder was committed at Pitlochry, which stands on the junction of the A9 and the A924, seven miles south-east of Blair Atholl in Perth.

History records that a certain Mrs Hays was waylaid and murdered in one of the nearby picturesque glens and, from that time onwards, her ghost has been seen haunting the spot. One of the best recorded sightings comes from the journal of Elizabeth Grant who, in the summer of 1886, was taking an evening stroll along one of the roads which winds through the glen between Pitlochry and Killiecrankie. Nothing disturbed her until she suddenly heard a deep groan behind her. On looking round she saw nothing at first, but then there gradually loomed before her a greenish spherical shape, illuminated from within, about the size of a large melon. It hovered on the top of the dyke skirting one side of the roadway.

Fascinated, yet quite frightened, Mrs Grant watched this

remarkable apparition which gradually formed itself into the head of a woman with long black hair, adorned with lace lappets or pearlins. The features were uncannily clear in the late evening light, and Mrs Grant recorded: 'I could see they were those of a person not of this earth. For a moment I did believe that a corpse had risen from the grave.'

The poor woman was terrified and stood fixed to the spot with her senses in a whirl. Then, with a tremendous effort of will she backed away a few paces. The head advanced along the top of the dyke for a few feet. Mrs Grant stepped further back but the sinister glowing head followed her. She tried to scream, but she couldn't, and then the apparition coupled with the uncanny silence became too much to bear and she began to walk hurriedly along the road.

She said: 'And so we went on, a procession of two, with the death's head sometimes gaining a yard, then me running and making a gap wider between us. Suddenly, at the termination of a wall, I saw that the head, which had appeared to be without a body and gliding along the top of the stones by itself was, in reality, attached to a filmy, wraith-like figure.'

The apparition then floated right across the road towards the terrified woman and, to her unspeakable horror, she saw the lashless eyelids slowly opening on the hideous face. At this she fainted out of sheer terror. She regained consciousness after a short time, and awoke to discover that the weird spectre had finally left her in peace and she stumbled home 'with the resolution fixed in my mind that never would I cross that way again'.

It would seem that Mrs Grant is not the only person to have had this terrifying experience. Shortly before the Second World War, a man in the neighbourhood saw – and hastily retreated from – the same corpse-like floating head. Whether it has been seen in recent years, I have been unable to discover.

Between May 1892 and August 1900, the figure of a ghostly clergyman was seen on several occasions in the village of St Boswells, on the B6398, about three miles south-east of Melrose.

This apparition was first seen by two sisters, Susan and Louisa Scott, between five and six o'clock in the evening. Having been for a short walk they were returning home when they saw, quite distinctly, the tall figure of a man dressed entirely in black. He wore a long coat, gaiters and knee-breeches. Round his throat was a white cravat and on his head he wore a low-crowned black hat. His face, which they only saw in profile, was exceedingly thin and deathly pale. The sisters stopped to let the figure pass them and, as he turned a bend in the road, his figure distinctly defined between the hedges, he suddenly evaporated into thin air.

About two months later, the sisters saw the figure again and without once taking their eyes off him, they watched until he again faded away near a small embankment. Without pausing for a moment, the two girls rushed frantically to either side of the road, but there was no sign of the man. They questioned two small boys who were on top of a haycart in the opposite field and to whom the whole road was clearly visible, but they were adamant that no one had passed that way.

On another occasion, the figure appeared to a group of village boys and, coming close up alongside them, instantly melted into thin air. Then, for a period of about two weeks, blue lights, moving in various directions, were seen after dark near the spot where the figure was most often seen. Some of the braver inhabitants of the village made attempts to follow them and solve the mystery, but their efforts proved fruitless.

Two schoolgirls from the village were picking wild strawberries, which grew on the bank where the figure disappeared. As they were gathering them, they heard a loud thud on the ground right beside them. Startled, they looked round, but seeing nothing, they continued to gather their strawberries. Then the sound was repeated and, looking up, they saw a tall thin man gazing intently at them. The girls fled in terror but, on reaching the safety of the village, looked back to see the figure still observing them. As they watched, he gradually faded away, as if enveloped in a vapour which suddenly grew around him.

In August 1894, the apparition was seen by a young governess who lived in the neighbourhood. She was walking home along the haunted road – the present B6398 – in the middle of the afternoon, when she saw in front of her a tall elderly man dressed in a long black cloak, with a cape which reached to just below his shoulders. His hat was low-crowned with the brim pulled over his eyes. Although frightened, the young woman did not take her eyes off the figure for one moment as she watched him walk backwards and forwards between the bend in the road and the bank. He did this for some time until he finally stopped, as if speaking to a man who was at that moment cutting one of the hedges.

What struck the young governess as peculiar, was the fact that the man cutting the hedge appeared quite unaware of the other's presence. She walked on, and was just about to pass the black figure when, to her astonishment, he vanished when she was less than three yards away. She was now so overcome with fear that she ran in hysterics to the nearest house.

Two other women reported seeing the figure in 1900. One, the lodge-keeper at Lossudden House, got a terrible fright when a man she had seen 'beyond the kirk' suddenly vanished. She said that she waited for the man expecting him to pass by, but he never did. 'He was' she said, 'the figure of the Devil, or a black man!'

My own enquiries into this apparition, which so far as I am aware has not been seen for the past eighty years, reveal that he is thought to be the ghost of a clergyman from St Boswells, from sometime in the eighteenth century. He is thought to have been responsible for the murder of his housekeeper, but I have not been able to discover his name, who his victim was, or just when the alleged murder took place. There does not appear to be anything covering the case in the local records either.

One bright summer afternoon, a party of villagers were returning by waggonette from Pitlochry to Killiecrankie and had just reached the Pass of Killiecrankie, some two miles north of Pitlochry on the present A9, when the horses started very violently, as if frightened by something. One of the passengers suddenly exclaimed: 'Good heavens! – What's that?'

The other passengers looked in the direction she had indicated and saw, standing a few yards away on a strip of grass, an extremely tall figure dressed in white, with a white cowl or hood drawn over its face. The figure stood still for several seconds and appeared to be watching the waggonette intently. Then it suddenly sprang forward racing after it in long loping strides. At this the horses, sensing danger, panicked and simply fled along the road and the passengers clung on like grim death to avoid being thrown off. Everyone on the waggonette was terrified as the figure chased after them, waving its arms as it did so and getting closer and closer.

But just as it got within reach, the horses gave a frantic leap forward and shot well ahead of it. To the intense relief of the passengers the figure stopped and stood motionless in the road, until a sudden bend hid it from view. On reaching Killiecrankie, they had recovered sufficiently enough to ask the driver if he could give any explanation for what had just happened, but he shook his head and said that every few years the apparition was seen hovering about the spot where they had just encountered it.

Another record tells of a young man who, while cycling on this road near the Pass of Killiecrankie, on his way home to the hamlet of Tummel Bridge, met the same figure, clad from head to foot in white. It bounded swiftly towards him and he, too nervous to investigate further, pedalled desperately in order to get away and avoid its grasp. According to local tradition, the white cowled figure is still sighted from time to time, yet no one seems to know who it represents or why it should haunt the road. Should the figure actually touch anyone unfortunate enough to meet it, that person is said to die within the year.

Travelling east from Aberdeen on the A944, you will pass on your left, about seven miles outside the town, the Loch of Skene. Here at Hogmanay, you are likely to encounter a spectral coach racing across the ice-cold waters of the loch, carrying the ghost of Alexander Skene, a local laird who lived in the area from 1680 to 1724.

Skene was interested in the black arts and, as a young man, he is said to have travelled to the Continent, where he remained for seven years studying black magic and witchcraft. On his return home he became known as the 'warlock laird', and it was said that when he went outdoors, even in the brightest sunlight, he never cast a shadow. He was often seen in the company of four imps, in the form of a crow, a hawk, a magpie and a jackdaw, and each Hogmanay, the birds would sit beside their master in his coach which was drawn by four black horses. He would drive to Skene churchyard, where the laird opened the newly filled graves of unbaptized babies, removing their little bodies which he then fed to his birds.

One old story, which gives rise to the alleged haunting, tells of how Alexander Skene crossed the loch, which bears his name, in his coach supported only by his magical powers. Hogmanay was chosen for this feat and the laird told his coachman to have his carriage ready and waiting by the door at midnight. It was a cold clear night but, as there was no frost, Skene cast a spell over the loch causing ice 'as thin as the finest glass', to form on the surface. Then, he told his coachman to keep the horses at full gallop during the crossing, and on no account to look behind him.

The carriage raced across the ice with the four birds flying alongside to encourage the horses. However, the terrified coachman could not stop himself from turning round just as the horses were within sight of the bank at the other side of Loch Skene. There, seated beside the laird was the Devil himself! In an instant, the back wheels of the coach smashed through the ice, just a few yards from the banks, throwing the coachman, the laird and the coach and horses into the icy waters of the loch.

Since that day, the spectral coach and horses are said to be seen racing across the loch each Hogmanay, and then disappearing just a few yards from safety.

Should you visit the village of Fordell, just off the A90 about six miles north of Kinross, you will be well advised to stay clear of the old village mill. Even today many local people avoid the ruined mill after dark, and some people are apprehensive about going near it alone even during the day.

In 1651, following the Battle of Pitreavie, Cromwell's victorious troops were quartered in the surrounding district. The miller at Fordell had a squad of Roundhead soldiers billeted with him who, despite his pleading, continually molested his wife and daughter. Out of sheer desperation, the miller killed the Roundheads by putting poison in their food and then he fled with his family.

A group of soldiers were sent to avenge their comrades but, being unable to find the miller or his wife and daughter, they arrested his assistant, Jock. Taking him outside the soldiers flogged him, before hanging him from the branch of an old oak tree which still stands today.

To this day it is said that at certain times and in certain seasons, Jock's ghost can still be seen hanging from the branch which creaks dolefully as his body swings to and fro. On some moonlit nights, Jock's ghostly corpse, with an agonised expression and staring eyes can be seen in the branches.

On the A967, four miles to the north of Stromness on mainland Orkney, you will find Clumly Farm, reputedly haunted by a ghostly white horse and its rider. The rider was a murderer, and his spirit is condemned to relive the terrible happenings of one particular night just over a century ago.

The story goes that a young woman from Loch of Stenness came to work at the farm. Two men working there took a fancy to her and soon became rivals for her favours. However, the girl – a flighty young thing, by all accounts – played one lover off against the other until the anguished men hated each other. One day, both men were threshing sheaves of oats and standing face to face across the barn floor with heavy flails in their hands. Suddenly one of them, perhaps goaded into fury by the taunts of the other, smashed his rival's skull with a blow from his flail, hiding the body in the barn.

Later that night, the murderer took a white horse from the stable, placed his victim's body across its back, and led the horse to the cliffs near Yescanaby where he threw the corpse into the Atlantic. As he left the scene, he was gripped by a terrible fear that the dead man's ghost was following him. He forced the horse into a wild gallop and, as he neared Clumly Farm, he jumped the beast over a dry-stone wall, but its hooves caught the top stones and brought them clattering down.

I have been unable to discover whether the murderer was caught and punished but, to this day, no one has been able to repair that broken section of the wall. As if it was a constant reminder of that terrible night, it always collapses again. On wild stormy nights in recent years, several people are said to have seen a ghostly white horse and its rider leap over the wall to the sound of falling stones. As recently as 1978, a woman living near Clumly Farm claimed to have answered a knock on her door only to find a white horse and rider standing outside. At her startled exclamation, the apparition promptly vanished.

Following any war, the true reckoning begins. The Jacobite Rebellion of 1745 ended in total failure for the Stuart cause. Bonnie Prince Charlie fled the country leaving his faithful Highlanders to suffer unspeakable wrongs at the hands of their English victors, under their cruel leader, the Duke of Cumberland. Cumberland was not called 'Butcher' for nothing. Under his leadership, murder, rape and house-burning were the order of the day and nothing was left undone that might break the proud spirit of the clans. They were forbidden to wear their traditional tartan, they could no longer carry swords, and they were not even allowed to play the bagpipes, which the English classified as a weapon of war.

But Highland blood is high, and the heaths and mountains hid as many broken and outlawed men as they did rabbits and foxes. Each had some vestige of a knife or rusted gun – and each had a hatred in his heart for the conquering Sassenachs.

On 28 September 1749, a party of soldiers led by Sergeant Arthur Davies of Guise's regiment, were optimistically ordered to join up with a patrol at Glenshee and then comb the area of ravines, mountains and bogs north of Perth. Davies was a modestly wealthy Englishman and something of a dandy, with silver buttons on his striped lute-string waistcoat, silver buckles on his brogues and his dark brown hair gathered into a silk ribbon. He also wore a silver watch and two gold rings, one of which had a peculiar distinguishing knob on it. He was in the habit of carrying a green silk purse, which on this occasion contained some fifteen gold guineas; a considerable amount in those days and no doubt suspected by the Highlanders to be loot.

Davies and his four men crossed the 2,200 foot Cairnwell Pass and descended into Glen Clunie where they surprised a man wearing a tartan coat. Davies should have arrested him, as tartan was looked on as military clothing, but by all accounts, he merely warned the stranger never to wear the coat again. Then Davies, who had always fancied himself as a sportsman, left his men temporarily because he thought he would like to cross the hill and try to get a stag. He said he would rejoin them later on their way to the rendezvous with the patrol. But he was never seen again, at least not in a mortal guise.

Then one night in June 1750, Davies's naked ghost appeared to Mistress Isobel MacHardie: 'Something naked that came in at the door and which frighted me so much I drew the clothes over my heid!' The ghost was seen on several occasions after that by various people, when it would call out to them, asking that his bones be located and given a decent Christian burial.

Two men were arrested for wearing tartan and they were found to have on them some of Davies's silver buttons and the gold rings. They were put on trial for his murder, but they were later aquitted for lack of sufficient evidence.

Today, the forlorn blue-coated ghost of Sergeant Arthur Davies can still occasionally be seen walking the Braemar hills and his unfortunate spirit still begs for a decent Christian burial.

Travel by ferry from Oban to Craignure on the Isle of Mull, and you will clearly see Duart Castle, perched high on the rocky edge of this moody and magnificent island. This is the ancestral home of the MacLeans of Duart and is now open to the public.

But few modern day visitors to this old impressive fortress will have caught a glimpse of the headless ghost of Ewen MacLean stalking the battlements or lofty stone-walled rooms, because the one-time clan chieftain much prefers to be seen riding his horse across the nearby dramatic Glen More, to the south of the island's highest peak, Ben More. Its craggy, remote country is, in winter, the ideal backcloth for any headless warrior.

Legend tells us that Ewen was a tall fearless warrior who was beheaded in battle. In 1558, Ewen and his father-in-law, The MacLean, had fallen out, and in the tradition of those days, it was decided that the issue should be settled on the battlefield. On the eve of the fight, Ewen was walking near Loch Scuabain when he encountered an old hag washing a bundle of bloodstained shirts in a stream.

He knew the creature for what she was and that the shirts belonged to doomed soldiers, and he wondered aloud if one of them was his. The hag replied that yes, one of them was his, but, she said: 'If your wife offers you bread and cheese with her own hand, without you asking for it, you will be victorious.'

The following dawn, Ewen buckled on his sword and waited anxiously for his wife to appear with some bread and cheese. But she didn't, and in the course of battle, Ewen was beheaded. His black horse is said to have galloped away with its headless rider still sitting upright in the saddle!

There is not even a footpath between Cape Wrath lighthouse and Sandwood Bay, only rocky hills and burns. The bay is the most north-westerly beach on the mainland of Great Britain and is situated about seven miles due south of the lighthouse, the nearest road being the A838, some seven miles to the south-east. It is known by the locals as the 'Land of Mermaids' and it is a perfect setting for such supernatural creatures. There is not

usually much sign of life here, and not much to see other than
sand, sea and dunes and the half-buried hulks of boats along the
beach.

Late one summer afternoon, a crofter and his son from nearby
Oldshore Mor, set out with their pony to gather driftwood from
the lonely Sandwood beach. They were the only human beings
for miles. As it began to grow dark, the pony became restless
and suddenly a bearded man, dressed in the uniform of a sailor,
appeared beside them and in a loud voice ordered the crofter
and his son to leave his property alone. Terrified they dropped
the wood on the sand and fled with their pony. So clearly did
they see this man before he vanished, clad in sea-boots, sailor's
cap and dark weather-beaten clothing, they could actually count
the brass buttons on his jacket.

Then in 1949, the ghostly sailor appeared to several members
of a fishing party and to a gillie from the Garbet Hotel in
Kinlochbervie, as they rounded one of the sand dunes. They all
saw him clearly as he traversed the crest of a sandy knoll with
his brass buttons glinting in the sunlight. Thinking he may have
been a poacher, the gillie went to question him, but when he
returned to the party his face was ashen and he said that there
was no one there at all, nor was there the faintest imprint of
footprints in the sand, other than his own.

Some years ago, three men from Kinlochbervie went to
Sandwood Bay in search of missing sheep. It was a fine night
with a bright moon as they walked along the seashore.
Approaching two large rocks they noticed some driftwood
coming in with the tide. Anxious to obtain some, one of the men
suggested he should scramble over the rock to try and secure a
fine plank that was floating there. Just as he set off, they all
distinctly saw the outline of a man standing on the sand
between the rocks.

When they approached the stranger, and saw his heavy
countenance and black whiskers, they stood rooted to the spot
in fear, for there was something unearthly about this huge man
who had suddenly materialized. Then, even as they watched,
the figure slowly walked behind a ledge of rock and
disappeared.

One afternoon in the summer of 1953, three visitors from
Edinburgh were picnicking on the sand-dunes to the south-east
of Sandwood Bay, when they saw a large bearded sailor gazing

down on them from the crest of a nearby hillock. They watched the figure for some minutes before it appeared to take several steps backwards and vanish without trace. Again, there were no footprints in the sand.

Just who the bearded sailor is, no one can be sure. Local belief is that it is the ghost of an Irish sea captain who was drowned off the coast here when his boat sank, and his body was washed ashore at Sandwood Bay.

# 6   Non-Paying Guests

To the inn comes the traveller in search of rest; the lonely in search of friendship; the sad in search of happiness and the poor in search of warmth. Add to these a murderer or two, a sprinkling of fugitives, a dash of plot and counter-plot and you have a rich breeding ground for ghost stories.

Isolated inns, of course, are more suited to such tales and many of them have a room, or rooms, which the ghost of some former occupant is supposed to visit. The old country inns set back from the lonely road deep in the heart of some bleak Highland glen, with its wooden sign swinging in the wind, the rusty hinges issuing ghostly creaks, creates just the right atmosphere for a haunting, be it fact or fiction.

On the remote shores of Loch Etive, to the north-west of Oban, there stands the lonely Highland Hotel, which from a distance looks more like some ancient castle than a place of rest and refreshment. It was here in the mid-1960s that two women tourists had a rather strange experience, which has yet to be satisfactorily explained.

The women were asked to share a very large room which contained two double beds, and which had two small windows overlooking the loch. As they had been on the road for several hours and were very tired, they went to bed quite early and were soon sound asleep. Then suddenly, one of the women was wakened by her friend urgently calling her name and saying that someone was trying to strangle her. She jumped out of bed and fumbled for the light switch but, on turning on the light, found the room empty except for her friend who was sitting up in bed with a look of terror on her face. The windows and door seemed secure so the two women decided that overtiredness and the unfamiliar surroundings had probably brought about a bad dream.

The following night they realized that the bedroom door would not lock properly and they decided it might be prudent to put something against it. So they dragged a very old and heavy oak carver chair over to the door and put it under the door handle to prevent anyone from entering. They didn't sleep too well on this occasion and during the night there seemed to be a terrible draught coming from somewhere. When they turned on the light, they were shocked to discover that the door was partly open. They shut it again and jammed the heavy chair back under the lock and, feeling more than a little nervous, decided to sleep together in one bed for mutual protection.

They also left the bedroom light on as an added precaution, and feeling more secure they drifted off into a fitful sleep. Then, at about half-past three in the morning, both women were suddenly awoken. They did not know what had wakened them, but inexplicably the room was icy-cold and their eyes were drawn to the door which, to their absolute horror, was slowly opening. The heavy chair proved to be no barrier as it was being pushed effortlessly back into the room. They could see no person, but a light, much brighter than the room light, seemed to float across the room and out of the far window. Plucking up their last reserves of courage, the women got out of bed and went on to the landing to see who was about – but it was empty and as silent as the grave.

At breakfast the next morning, they mentioned their experience to the hotel manager and were given what might be a possible explanation as to what caused their sleepless night. It appears that the old hotel had once been a castle, built on the site of an earlier fortification and the owner had married an Irish princess back in the Middle Ages.

The princess had four brothers and they, disapproving of the girl's marriage, came to take her back to the Emerald Isle. This they did, but in the resultant fight her husband was killed, and it is thought to be her ghost which comes back from time to time to look for her lost love.

It is not recorded whether the two women spent another night in the room.

At Bridge of Earn, on the A90 about four miles from Perth, you will find the Moncrieffe Arms, a pub which has a long history of haunting and where, over the years, a number of visitors have experienced unusual noises on the upper floors.

During the 1970s, a new landlord took over the premises and not entirely believing in the existence of ghosts, he tried to find a logical explanation for the inexplicable sound of footsteps and crying, which seemed to come from one of the upper corridors. His scepticism turned to belief when a strange incident occurred in the bathroom.

The landlord, wanting to use the room, went upstairs and attempting to open the bathroom door found it locked. From inside he could hear the sound of splashing water, as if someone was taking a bath. The landlord didn't think anything of it at first and he began to walk away, but then, looking back he saw the bathroom door was now wide open and, when he went in, both the bath and the towels were completely dry. Later he was to discover that no one had been near the bathroom for well over an hour!

When it comes to Bonnie Prince Charlie, it only needs a faint whiff of history or the mere shadow of a legend to conjure him into a fully-fledged member of the spectral community. In 1745, he is reputed to have stayed for a short time at the County Hotel in Dumfries.

There is a well-known story about a visitor sitting in the upstairs lounge, some time in the early 1930s, who claims to have seen a male figure, dressed in a kilt and the clothes of the Jacobite period, slowly emerge through a disused doorway. He stood there for a few minutes deep in thought and with a worried look on his face. The figure then turned and went out through the same disused door.

It was only the next day the visitor learned that the upper lounge is known as 'Bonnie Prince Charlie's Room'. These were his quarters in 1745 and he is said to have slept at the other side of the disused door through which his ghost appeared. What makes this story a little doubtful is that, so far as I am aware, the phantom does not seem to have made another appearance since.

At Arrochar, a small community at the junction of the A85 and the A814, at the northern tip of Loch Long, they boast of an eighteenth-century hotel built as a domestic residence by a man called Colquhoun. It was in the hands of the Colquhoun family until quite recently.

The story which surrounds this haunting goes back to the end of the eighteenth century when the Highlands were just beginning to settle down again after the savage repression, which followed the '45 Rebellion. Colquhoun set off early one morning to walk to Luss, some ten miles to the south on the shores of Loch Lomond, on business. (Luss stands on the present A82.) After walking a few miles, Colquhoun realized he had forgotten some important papers and, feeling a bit irritable at having done so, he turned back towards his home at Arrochar.

His irritation turned to outrage when he entered his house and found his wife naked in bed with a neighbour. Blind with rage, he stabbed his wife with his dirk and she, although fatally wounded, dragged herself along the upper passageway into one of the bedrooms, where she died. The neighbour died where he lay with Colquhoun's dirk implanted in his chest. The slaughter took less than two minutes but, for the next twenty-four hours, Colquhoun wandered through the house in agonies of remorse until, unable to withstand the guilt a moment longer, he hanged himself.

From that time onwards, it is believed that the ghost of the dead woman makes her presence felt – although she has never been seen – whenever a death is about to occur in the family. This is something which was certainly borne out about thirty years ago, when the proprietor's brother was killed in a road accident.

I am told that, at that time, the hotel was still in the hands of the Colquhoun family and several guests were staying there. One morning, one of the guests asked Mr Colquhoun if the place was haunted. The guest explained that on the previous night as he walked along the top corridor to his room, on his way to bed, he became aware that someone was following him. He turned round thinking it was another guest, but was surprised to discover that the corridor behind him was empty. Assuming he had been mistaken, he continued towards his room and was immediately aware of the presence again. Almost at once, an invisible person walked past him and it seemed as if it turned into one of the rooms as he passed.

It was just twenty-four hours later that the proprietor's brother was killed in a road accident.

At the turn of the century, a waiter at the Palace Hotel in Aberdeen, a man not easily upset by strange circumstances, suddenly quit his job because of the ghostly activities which were said to have been going on there at the time.

He told a local investigator that the staff had, for some days, been disturbed by a strange knocking on the windows downstairs late at night. As a result, they had arranged that they would sit up one night, and that half of the men would remain at the windows to pull up the shutters when the knocking began, and the other half would be gathered around the doors ready to rush out and seize anyone they saw.

Just before midnight, the usual knocking was heard on the windows and the blinds were immediately pulled up and, the waiter along with all the other men at the windows, saw the naked figure of a man drift quickly across the road. The men stationed at the door rushed after it, but they were unable to catch up with the figure before it mysteriously disappeared. One thing they did notice, however, was that the fleeing man left no footprints in the freshly fallen snow.

No one today knows who, or what, caused the haunting or why the naked figure persistently hammered on the windows and, so far as I know, there have been no further occurrences since.

On the wooded slopes of the north-western shores of Loch Ness, Aultsigh stands on the A82, about ten miles north-west of Fort Augustus. The Aultsigh Inn – sometimes known as 'Halfway House' – is a blissful place to stay overnight or ideal as a base from which to explore this beautiful part of the Highlands. Unless, that is, you have the misfortune to be accommodated in the haunted bedroom.

The story behind the haunting is that two brothers, Malcolm and Alasdair Macdonnell, both fell in love with the same beautiful girl, Annie Fraser, who lived at nearby Grota, and to whom both brothers had made love on several occasions. One night, Alasdair and Annie met in a grove near the Aultsigh Burn, a picturesque stream which runs along the boundary between Urquhart and Glenmorriston, some two miles away.

They had climbed to a small cairn on the western shoulder of Mealfourvounie but, unknown to them, Malcolm Macdonnel had followed them and cruelly interrupted their surreptitious love-making by bursting out of his hiding place, brandishing a dirk. After challenging his brother, a fierce struggle took place while the girl, white and shaking, called first to one and then to the other in an effort to stop the fighting. Neither man took any notice of the girl's pleas and eventually Malcolm overcame his brother with a powerful thrust of his dirk which plunged into Alasdair's chest, killing him instantly. After throwing the body into a gully, he then turned his attention to Annie Fraser and, disregarding her cries for mercy, he strangled her and hid her body until darkness fell.

In the dead of night Malcolm returned to the hiding place and retrieved the girl's body and dragged it down the track of the burn to the cottage, which is now the Aultsigh Inn. There he hid the pathetic remains under the floorboards of what was, at that time, a disused room. Collecting all his valuables and a bag of gold, Malcolm set off to cross Loch Ness. For some reason or other, just before he reached the safety of the opposite shore, his frail boat sank and he was drowned.

Over the years there have been a number of incidents in the Aultsigh Inn, and several visitors have testified to hearing footsteps in the still of the night. These sounded as if someone was moving slowly and methodically backwards and forwards across the haunted room tirelessly searching for something. No one can say for sure whether this is the ghost of Malcolm or Alasdair Macdonnell, for the unknown ghost has never been seen. However, there are a number of stories circulating in the area which tell of the ghost of Annie Fraser – a girl with flashing eyes and beautiful raven hair – who haunts both the Aultsigh Inn and the surrounding district.

About two hundred years ago, a ship was wrecked on the rocks at Eddrachillis Bay, some thirty miles to the south of Cape Wrath on the north-west tip of Scotland. Some days after the wreck, a barrel of whisky was washed ashore at Kerrachar Bay in Loch Cairnbawn.

This barrel of whisky was discovered by a local fisherman called Tordeas, who carried it to the old ferryhouse at Kylesku – now the Kylesku Ferry Inn – which stands, as its name implies, at the ferry berth on the A894.

After depositing the barrel and its precious contents in an upstairs room of the inn – a room which can still be seen if you are prepared to climb a wooden loft ladder to view it – Tordeas invited some of his friends to come and share the contents with him.

During the drunken orgy that followed, a 'seer' who was present prophesied a great calamity, which was greeted with ridicule by the other men present. A drunken argument followed which became so heated, Tordeas had to protest that 'the hour was drawing near to the Lord's Day'. In other words it was nearly Saturday midnight.

Tordeas's son, more drunk than the rest, lost his temper and attacked his father for wanting to break up the party. In the fight which inevitably ensued, he threw Tordeas down the ladder breaking his neck. Before he died, Tordeas screamed out in agony: 'My son, I shall return to have my revenge on thee!'

This revenge held good for many years, as each year at midnight on the anniversary of his death, Tordeas's ghost was said to appear at the entrance to the hotel's snug, just below the loft ladder leading to the room where the drunken fight took place. I am told that the last time he was clearly seen and his appearance recorded was by the late Professor C.M. Joad in about 1950.

In 1885, Revd Joseph Murphy and his wife were touring Scotland and found themselves in Dundee without a room for the night. After making enquiries, they found themselves a room at a delightful sixteenth-century inn, on the Perth road, which was a welcoming gabled structure with projecting windows. Inside they found the rooms were large and well kept, with low ceilings and floors and there were oak-panelled walls and an oak staircase. The diamond-latticed windows, narrow passages, nooks and crannies and old cupboards all provided a quaint but comfortable atmosphere.

Despite this, however, Mrs Murphy appeared to have certain misgivings about the room they were given, which was at the rear of the inn at the end of a long panelled passage and overlooking the yard and stables. It was a big room with a huge four-poster bed and well-aired sheets, and the remainder of the furnishings were comparable with the majority of well-run hotels of the day. But, in this room, there was a strange dark cupboard set deep into the wall, facing the bed, which appeared rather unusual and out of place.

Tired after a long day, they undressed and prepared for bed. Blowing out the candle, Revd Murphy wished his wife goodnight and almost immediately went off to sleep. She, on the other hand, was unable to sleep due to the fact that she was spending the night in a strange bed in strange surroundings – an experience shared by many readers, I'm sure. She lay listening to her husband gently snoring beside her, wishing she could get to sleep herself, when suddenly she became aware of a smell – an offensive, pungent smell which blew across the room.

At first, Mrs Murphy could not locate the source but, as the smell kept wafting in her nostrils, she gradually became convinced that it was originating from the big cupboard opposite the bed. Unable to stand it any longer, she quietly slipped out of bed and crept across to the cupboard in the gloom. Every step she took increased the foul smell and, by the time she reached the cupboard, she felt suffocated by it. Nervously, she reached out and opened the cupboard door and, as she did so, a faint glow seemed to fill the room and she saw, in front of her, a human head floating in mid-air!

Terrified, yet unable to cry out, she stared at it open-mouthed. It was the head of a man with a matted crop of short reddish hair that fell over the upper part of his forehead and ears. All else seemed to be lost in a disgusting mass of decomposing flesh. Then the horrifying thing began to move slowly towards her and with a scream, she fled to the bed and began to shake her husband awake. By this time the head was close to them and had she not dragged her bemused husband out of the way, it would have touched them.

Revd Murphy seized his walking stick and lashed out at it with all his might, but the stick met no resistance and the head continued its advance. Then the terrified couple made a frantic attempt to find the door as the head followed them. Bumping into something in the semi-darkness, Revd and Mrs Murphy both fell over and landed in a heap on the floor. The head approached and hovered over them, before slowly descending lower and lower until it had passed right through Revd Murphy and out of sight through the floor.

It was only much later that they were to discover the probable cause of their frightening experience. Sometime in the eighteenth century, a pedlar had been murdered at the inn and his decapitated body was hidden behind the wainscoting. His head had been put under the floor of the cupboard in the room the Murphys had occupied. The murderer or murderers were never found but are thought to have been drowned when a ship, on which they were hoping to escape, sank just after leaving the port of Dundee.

The White Dove Hotel in Aberdeen was the scene of some rather remarkable events which have never been fully explained.

One day, a very attractive young woman booked into the hotel under the name of Miss Vining. On arrival she looked unwell and within two days she was to complain of feeling ill and asked for a doctor to attend her. A local GP was summoned and he diagnosed that she was suffering from a rare tropical disease. Because of the severity of her condition, the doctor would not allow her to be removed to Aberdeen hospital. Instead she was to be isolated in her room and two nurses were sent from the hospital to care for her round the clock.

On the second night, one of the nurses had been sitting with the desperately ill woman for about two hours and, after taking her temperature, she had settled down to read a book. Glancing up, she saw to her surprise that the chair beside the patient's bed was occupied by a tiny little girl. How she had managed to get into the room unnoticed the nurse could not understand, but she assumed that the wind howling across the chimneys had deadened the sound of the door and her footsteps.

The nurse rose from her chair and was about to tell the child to go, when the girl raised a small hand and waved her back. The nurse was spellbound by the child's action for some reason and she stood staring at her, tongue-tied and trembling.

The child wore a very wide-brimmed hat which hid her facial features, but from her graceful little figure and dainty limbs, she appeared to be quite pretty and had an aristocratic look about her. Her dress, though not of the best quality, was far from cheap and there was something about its style that suggested it was of foreign origin.

On duty the next night, during which time the wind had dropped and there had been a heavy fall of snow, the nurse made sure that she locked the door to keep out unwanted visitors. At about one o'clock she was dozing in the chair when she was roused by a fearful and agonized cry from her dangerously ill patient. She looked across and saw, seated in the same position as on the previous night, the small child. The nurse sprang to her feet and with a gasp of amazement lunged towards the child who, as before, raised her hand. The nurse collapsed back into her chair, paralysed.

Her patient was moaning and groaning in pain, yet she was unable to attend to her, being incapable of movement. She could only sit and listen. Every second the patient's condition grew worse, each groan sounding as if another nail had been hammered in her coffin. Then, after what seemed an eternity, the child rose from the chair with her head bowed and moved slowly from the bed towards the window. The spell was broken and the nurse, with an angry cry, quickly got up and faced the little intruder.

She snatched at the child's hat which melted away in her hands and to her unspeakable horror, she found herself looking into the face of a corpse. The figure was that of a Hindu child with a big gaping slit across her throat. The nurse promptly fainted. On recovering the nurse found that the ghostly visitor had gone and that her patient had died. During her last moments the woman had thrown one hand across her eyes, as if trying to shut out some object which she was afraid to look at. Her other hand grasped the counterpane.

No one knows what the relationship was between Miss Vining and the young Hindu child and, as far as I am aware, the tiny ghost was never seen again. But for a long time afterwards, the White Dove Hotel was haunted by a woman thought to be the ghost of Miss Vining.

Not far from Port Ellen, on the A846 on the Island of Islay, there stands a large private hotel, which has been converted from an old distillery.

A male visitor staying here, earlier this century, was on his way upstairs to bed with a candle in his hand, when he saw a figure some paces ahead of him, walking in the same direction. From the appearance of the figure, he knew it could not be his host who was a tall man. The person in front of him was a short thick-set man and was dressed in what he later described as 'antiquated garb'. For several seconds he watched the figure which then appeared to melt into thin air at the end of the passage. Its disappearance was followed by what sounded like a dull, heavy thud and then absolute silence. Frightened, the guest lost no time in getting to his room and securely locking the door behind him.

That night, the man had a most vivid dream. He felt that someone, or something, was drawing him towards a high window at the end of the passage. Struggle as he might, he could not escape. In his dream he caught at the furniture, the curtains and anything else he could grab at to stop himself being drawn further towards the window. Then he saw himself on the window-ledge peering down into a sickening gulf. He felt himself falling and then suddenly, he woke up with a start to hear a clock striking five.

Dismissing it as a bad dream, he said nothing to his host but, on the following night as he was going to bed, he was again unnerved to see the same shadowy figure preceding him along the corridor, which vanished again on reaching the blank wall at the end of it. Again there was a heavy thud followed by an ominous silence. Again he dreamed the same dream, finding himself moving step by step towards an open window. The sensation was so vivid he woke up – only to find himself at the end of the passage leading from his room and pressing with both hands against the blank wall.

He had never walked in his sleep before and, quite upset by the experience, he mentioned it to his host the next morning. He was told that at some time in the early nineteenth century, before the modern section of the distillery building had been erected, a man had broken in at the dead of night and, thinking himself in seventh heaven, set about trying to drink the place dry!

Now, we all know that the odd dram or two of the amber nectar does a power of good. But when you down two or three bottles of even the finest whisky in a couple of hours, as this man did, you find yourself in deep trouble. Under the influence of the liquor he could not find his way out of the distillery and mistook the second floor window for the door, calmly staggering through and falling to his death on the cobbles below.

The window has since been walled up and the modern part of the building added at the end of the corridor. The apparition was well known to be the earthbound spirit of the man who had crashed to his death almost one hundred years before, and it is alleged that the distillery is still haunted by his ghost to this very day.

The Kingshouse Hotel stands on the A82 not far from Glen Coe, some twelve miles north of Bridge of Orchy.

One autumn afternoon, a tourist set out from the hotel to walk to Rannoch. He quite obviously did not realise the treacherous nature of the ground, nor the time it would take to complete his journey. By the time he had reached the eastern end of Loch Laidon he was tired and footsore. All afternoon he had not encountered a living soul, but he plodded on concentrating on keeping a foothold on the narrow twisting path on the north side of the loch.

Just as he was rounding a large boulder, with treacherous bog on either side of him, he became aware of the sound of heavy footsteps coming from behind. He thought that perhaps another hiker or a keeper was approaching him. As the footsteps drew closer and louder, he began to experience a sense of fear, for accompanying the footsteps he could also make out the eerie sound of rattling chains. A cool breeze began to blow and for some reason he felt afraid to look back.

The steps grew closer and closer until he sensed that someone was at his heels and then alongside him. When he forced himself to look and see who it might be, he saw a tall grey man with a grotesquely shaped head, out of all proportion to the size of his body, walk past him with a strange sliding movement and without saying a word. He could not help but notice the egg-shaped head, with its wrinkled cheeks and forehead which were covered with black spots, rather like large freckles. The ears were large and under a thick mane of black matted hair and his eyes were wild and saucer like.

Badly shaken, the tourist stumbled on behind the apparition which then disappeared from view behind a large rock a few hundred feet ahead and was soon lost in the mist which had begun to descend.

The tourist decided to turn back to the Kingshouse Hotel. He was extremely tired, lonely and scared. He had not met a soul along this god-forsaken road across Rannoch Moor and by the time he reached a little bridge over a stream, he felt desperate for company of any sort. Then he saw, sitting on the parapet of the bridge and silhouetted in the moonlight, the figure of an old man, whom he felt sure must be a gamekeeper. As he approached a chill wind began to blow and the moon slid behind a cloud, although it was bright enough to show the dim outline of the bridge and the old man sitting on the parapet.

The tourist went straight up to the old gentleman and, in no time at all, had begun a friendly conversation. He told him of his experience and said how he had been frightened when a monstrous-looking man with a huge egg-shaped head overtook him on the moorland. Did the old gentleman know who he might be? The old man remained silent beside him. He seemed strangely quiet but, when the moon reappeared from behind the cloud, the old man turned to face him displaying his egg-shaped head with its coarse black mane and tiny horns protruding from the temples! The last thing the tourist said he remembered, was that the face wore a devilishly cunning smile.

While researching this book, the author had occasion to spend a couple of nights in a certain hotel in the centre of Edinburgh. It is a typical Edwardian hotel which, like many today, has lost much of its former elegance under several layers of paint, false walls and modern bar fittings. Although it must be said that the public loo on the ground floor was a splendid example of Edwardian architecture and one of the finest I have ever seen.

My bedroom was at the end of a corridor on the second floor and, as it was a corner room, I was able to obtain a fine view of two of the city's elegant streets. Apart from that it was just like any other hotel bedroom: functional, overheated and with a bed that would have slept four others beside me.

On my second night there, having tramped just about every pavement in the city, I was worn out so after dinner and a couple of pints in the hotel bar, I decided that I would have what was for me, at least, a reasonably early night as I had to catch a train early the following morning. I lay in bed reading for about half an hour or so and suddenly I heard a light tap on the door. Actually I thought it was on the door of the room next to mine and ignored it at first, until it happened again, this time a little louder. I called out: 'Come in', but nothing happened. After several seconds there was another knock on the door and again I called out for whoever was there to come in. Then thinking I might have put the dead-latch down on the lock, I got out of bed and opened the door only to find no one there. I looked along the corridor, but that was empty too and as the stairs and the lift were at the other end it was not possible, I thought, for anyone to have reached either of them in the time it took me to open the door.

Thinking to myself that all this ghost-hunting was finally beginning to get to me, I shrugged it off, closed the door and got back into bed. The next morning I was up quite early and, after paying my bill, had a half-hour to spare so I sat in the empty foyer reading the morning paper. The manager, or the assistant manager, appeared and on seeing me came across for a few words. Was everything to my satisfaction? Had I been comfortable? etc. I asked him if anyone had been trying to contact me the previous night and, when he said that they would have telephoned my room from reception, I mentioned the curious incident of the knocks on my bedroom door.

He went quiet for a moment. Then he said: 'Are you sure, sir? Someone knocked on your door?' Now this man did not know me, what I did, or why I was in Edinburgh. No one in the hotel did, as far as I am aware, so I'm sure that there had been no deliberate attempt to set me up in any way. I really had to press him to tell me what was wrong and reluctantly he said in a quiet voice: 'That would have been "Aggie", sir.' After pressing him further and promising that if ever I mentioned the story to anyone I would not name the hotel or the road where it stands, he agreed to giving me a brief outline as to who 'Aggie' was.

It would appear that 'Aggie' (I have changed the name of the ghost) is the hotel's resident spectre; a former maid who was induced to meet a guest in the room I had occupied quite by coincidence, sometime between the wars. By all accounts she must have been a bit naïve, for when the guest began making advances towards her, she objected and to stop her screaming the man had strangled her. Although to my knowledge 'Aggie' has never actually been seen, since that time several guests have frequently remarked on the knocking on their door late at night – and they have all been male guests on their own.

# 7 Mysterious, Unexplained Phenomena

Most apparitions appear to have some reason to haunt a particular spot and historical records can usually be discovered to give at least a possible explanation of the haunting. However, there are many well authenticated sightings of ghosts which cannot be accounted for and remain as mysterious today as they were at the time they were experienced.

One misty morning in the spring of 1884, the late Professor John Collie, Professor of Organic Chemistry at London University, was climbing alone up the 4,300 foot Ben Macdhui, in the Cairngorm Mountains.

Slowly and carefully he made his way over the snow-covered ground of the last few hundred feet to the flat summit. The snow was crisp and visibility was down to no more than about twenty yards. On reaching the summit, Professor Collie, then only a young man in his mid-twenties, stopped for a short breather by the cairn which was set up there in 1847 by an Ordnance Survey team. Having rested and breakfasted on a bar of chocolate and a few nuts, he walked away from the cairn and into the mist. He had not gone very far when he heard the sound of crunching snow behind him, as if someone was following him and taking long loping strides.

Assuming another climber was behind him in the thick mist, Collie waited for the man to catch up with him but the moment he stopped, so did the footsteps. Thinking it was his imagination, he walked on again, and the footsteps crunched on the hard snow behind him. He heard them more clearly now and they appeared to be getting closer. Again he stopped walking, but could still see no one.

Shrugging off the uneasy feeling which had by now come over him, Collie set off again but, as before, when he moved away the eerie crunch of the footsteps began again very close behind him. Yet still he could see nothing in the mist. Suddenly he was terror-stricken but he could not understand why as he had never minded being alone on the mountain before. He took to his heels and ran, staggering blindly down the mountain-side. It was only after he had reached the reassuring safety of his lodgings that he managed to pull himself together.

Then, in June 1890, a Doctor Kellas and his younger brother were on Ben Macdhui late one evening. The brother had climbed to the summit and Doctor Kellas had spent some time on a slope on the fold of the hill, well below the cairn, looking for minerals. Looking up, he saw the figure of a man come up through one of the passes and wander slowly round the stone cairn, near which his brother was now sitting. Kellas was surprised, for it was getting quite late for anyone to be wandering alone on the top of Ben Macdhui. But his surprise turned to astonishment when he saw that the man was nearly the same height as the cairn, which is some ten feet tall. As he watched, the large figure, after circling the cairn, slowly descended into the same pass it had just emerged from and disappeared.

Doctor Kellas ran to his brother who was still sitting by the cairn and asked him who the man was who had been walking round him. His brother looked up puzzled and replied: 'What man? I never saw anyone!' A cold unnatural fear now gripped both men and they quickly descended the mountain.

Today, no one can account for the mysterious figure but, among the members of the Cairngorm Mountain Rescue Team, he is known as the 'Ferla Mhor' or 'Big Grey Man'. They will tell you that he is still glimpsed on the odd occasion by climbers and is well known among the older Speyside residents. But the riddle of Ben Macdhui still remains. When Professor Collie died in 1942, he remained convinced to the end that there was some horrifying supernatural phenomenon on the summit of the mountain, and nothing would have induced him to go back up there again.

In 1955, the aircraft carrier HMS *Glory* was undergoing a refit in Rosyth Dockyard. It was just after the Christmas holidays when a painter boarded her alone at about half-past seven one cold morning. He made his way to a cabin on the gallery deck where he kept his working clothes. Just outside the cabin was a locker where he kept his lamp, which he needed when he worked in the long dark alleyways. This was a double lamp which would light both the cabin and the alleyway, and he stepped inside the cabin to plug it in.

When the light was turned on, the painter was surprised to see a tall man dressed in a tropical flying kit and standing near the dressing table in the cabin. He wore a pair of blue shorts and a leather RAF flying jacket with a fur collar. He had a flying helmet on the back of his head and had a wave of hair sticking out. But most noticeable was the long angry red scar on the side of his neck.

The painter and the flyer stared at each other for a moment and then, thinking he might be a member of the ship's naval maintenance staff still aboard the carrier, the painter said: 'Good morning. Did you have a nice Christmas?' The figure didn't reply. The painter stepped out of the cabin to get his jacket out of the locker, when it suddenly struck him as rather peculiar that anyone should be in the cabin in full flying kit. He turned round to ask the man who he was, but the cabin was empty.

He grabbed the lamp which he had hung above the door and rushed back into the small cabin to search it. There was only a bunk, a dressing table and an open locker which were all empty and no sign of anyone in the cabin. Overcome with fear, the painter dropped his lamp and rushed along the alleyway shouting. As he plunged down the companion-way he was stopped by a workmate, who saw what a state he was in, and together they returned to the cabin to examine it again, but found nothing or no one. The painter had to be taken off the ship in a state of shock.

News of the spectral pilot reached the ears of the Naval authorities who ordered the ship's commander to instigate a thorough search of the vessel, but no sign of the phantom pilot could be found. It wasn't long before the rumour swept the dockyard that HMS *Glory* was haunted by an apparition, and it was suggested that it was the ghost of a pilot who had been killed when he crash-landed on the flight deck during the Korean War, round about Christmas time. However, the naval authorities claim that there have been no previous sightings aboard HMS *Glory*, and although there had been considerable loss of life among the pilots during her service in Korean waters, none had died as a result of crash-landing on the carrier's flight deck. Neither was it possible that the apparition was that of an RAF officer, as no RAF personnel had ever served aboard the ship. So, whoever the ghost was or why he haunted HMS *Glory* still remains a mystery.

Mention of HMS *Glory* brings to mind a haunting which took place on board the square-rigger *The Lady of Avenel,* when she lay idle at Leith during the winter of 1933. She had a rather strange history. She was built at Falmouth in 1875, sailed just about every square inch of ocean on earth with a variety of cargoes, and was rumoured to have been used in running slaves from Africa at one stage of her life. Twice she had sailed round the Cape and on at least two Arctic expeditions, the last in 1925.

Following this Arctic voyage, when she was almost trapped in the ice, she was sold and renamed the *Island* and almost immediately became haunted by the mysterious ghost of a woman, who was often seen roaming her decks, both when she was at sea and when she was in port. Because of her ghostly reputation, and seamen being a superstitious breed anyway, there was great difficulty in crewing her. As a result she was again renamed, this time as the *Virgo* but, instead of putting a stop to the hauntings, this only seemed to make them worse.

On her final voyage as the *Virgo,* the crew had a few very unnerving experiences. One sailor, who claimed to know nothing of the ghost, was reading in his bunk, when the empty bunk opposite began to shake violently. On another occasion, a crewman was reading in his bunk after coming off watch one night, when the oil-lamp suddenly went dim. He thought the oil had run out but, when he checked, he discovered the lamp had only recently been filled. He turned the wick up and went back to his reading, but had to give up when, time after time, the lamp dimmed. Then, as the man was about to get his head down for the night, he was terrified to see a ghostly form which stretched out a long arm and turned the lamp up!

Another seaman went to sleep with a torch under his pillow. He woke up with a start when the light from it was shone in his face. The man swore it was impossible for the torch to have been turned on by accident. It seems that this happened to him on several nights running, following which the poor man had a nervous breakdown and had to be put ashore at the next port of call.

One day, round about the midday watch change, the ship's skipper heard footsteps on the deck above him. Although the watch was due to change, there should not have been any one on this deck and so he went to check. There was no one there but, as he came out of the hatchway and on to the deck, he heard a woman's voice coming from the poop deck behind him, although he knew that there was no woman on board.

Eventually, after further ghostly goings-on, the ship docked at Leith where the crew were no doubt relieved to be paid off, and the ship lay idle for some time after being put up for sale. One night the watchman, who was alone on board, found it difficult to get to sleep. He was sitting up in his bunk reading, when suddenly he saw the ghost of a woman walk through the wooden bulkhead and go out again through the closed cabin door. The terrified watchman resigned on the spot and no other watchman would stay on the ship alone after that.

In time the ship was bought by the Royal Yorkshire Yacht Club for conversion into a luxury yacht. One of the very first things they did was to give the ship her original name back – *The Lady of Avenel*. This appears to have satisfied the mysterious female ghost, for the hauntings ceased almost at once.

There is a Gaelic word, *Taradh*, which loosely translated means something like 'an influence unconsciously exerted by the strong emotions of another'. This can be illustrated by an incident concerning the singer Mabel Mercer, which took place in Glasgow during the Great War and which has never been fully explained. The full details of the case are in the records of the Clydeside Public Libraries and only an outline is given here.

Miss Mercer was only fifteen years old at the time and was making her showbiz début at the Glasgow Empire in a music hall act with her aunt. When they were between jobs on one occasion, she and her aunt were invited to dine with a lady who lived in one of the wealthy residential suburbs of the city. It was 1915 and all around lay evidence that Britain was at war with the Kaiser's Germany.

Their hostess lived in a very large late Georgian house which had a wide front hall with a fireplace and was carpeted throughout. The ladies had a leisurely dinner following which coffee was served in the sitting-room. At approximately ten o'clock, Miss Mercer and her aunt were about to leave, when their hostess said that she must post a letter to her husband who was serving somewhere abroad with the British Army, although she had no idea just where.

As it was a mild night, their hostess suggested that she might walk with them as far as the post box, a few hundred yards from the house. They were just about to open the front door, when they heard the sound of marching feet, a sound which was immediately recognised in 1915 as the unmistakable rhythmic, scuffling step of marching troops.

The hostess was quite surprised since, so far as she knew, there were no troops stationed in that part of Glasgow at the time and, as the docks were over on the opposite side of the city, there was little possibility that they were troops about to embark for France. As the women commented on this, the sound grew louder and louder, as if the marching troops were coming nearer. All three women rushed outside to see the passing soldiers, but were astonished to discover that on opening the wide front door everything was silent outside. There was neither sight nor sound of the marching troops, or anything else to disturb the silence of that suburban neighbourhood.

Baffled, they went back into the house, where they had an even greater surprise; the sound of marching feet could still be heard and it was louder than before. In fact, it was almost deafening and the vibration actually shook the floor. Even the large heavy oak table in the hall was quivering. The women stood almost petrified with a mixture of fear and bewilderment, until gradually the sound faded away in the distance – exactly as it does when a regiment of soldiers has passed out of sight and hearing.

The hostess asked Miss Mercer and her aunt if they would accompany her down the street. They found a policeman and asked him if he had seen the marching soldiers. But he told them that he had been on duty for several hours, and he knew of no troop movements in the vicinity. Certainly none had passed him.

To this day the events remain a mystery, but perhaps the hostess's letter to her husband, and the thoughts contained in it, had somehow bridged the gap between them. Who knows?

One of the weirdest tales I came across during my research for this book concerns William Craighead who, in the middle of the nineteenth century, was the schoolmaster at Monifieth on the Tay estuary, some six miles east of Dundee. At the time these events took place, William Craighead was a young man and something of a practical joker who was not particularly scrupulous about the means or the consequences of his jokes – just so long as they were not played on him.

A man had died in the area and, as is the Celtic custom, there was a wake, to which Craighead and a number of his friends had been invited. Yet, even under these circumstances, the young schoolmaster could not restrain himself from performing a practical joke. He arranged with one of his close friends to get all the 'watchers' out of the house or, at least, out of the room where the corpse was laid out in its coffin.

Having succeeded in this, Craighead removed the body from the coffin and placed it in an outhouse, while another member of his group of friends took the corpse's place in the coffin. The whole idea of this rather nauseating practical joke was for the mourners to return to the room and, at a signal from Craighead, the imposter, shrouded like the dead man, would rise from his coffin accompanied by suitable moans and groans and terrify the assembled guests.

So, having placed the real corpse in the outhouse, Craighead returned to the house and mingled with the other mourners. After they had again been seated in the room containing the 'corpse' and their glasses had been refilled, the signal was given for the shrouded 'corpse' to rise. But there was no response. The signal was again given and, to Craighead's surprise, was completely ignored. Slightly alarmed, he thought it was just possible that his fellow trickster had fallen asleep in the coffin and he went over to give him a nudge. He was horrified, however, to see when he looked into the coffin that the man appeared to be dead!

I suppose one should show a little charity and feel sorry for the schoolmaster. His feelings can well be imagined and he had no option but to disclose the dreadful fact to the grieving relatives. One can imagine their reactions also, and the problem was hardly alleviated when every attempt to restore the thoughtless young imposter in the coffin proved abortive.

Then someone suddenly realized that the original corpse was missing and Craighead, now suitably humbled and subdued, went to the outhouse with another mourner to recover it – only to find it had disappeared. The alarm and anger of the family now redoubled and when knowledge of the whereabouts of the corpse was denied by all those present, the situation in the house can more easily be imagined than described. Craighead himself was on the verge of collapse by this time.

When daylight came, there was still no trace of the corpse and Craighead was accused of being the prime culprit in its disappearance – something he vehemently denied. He was now so affected by what had happened that he was incapable of sleep and wandered the area for several days and nights in search of the missing body. In the event, it was discovered by some farm workers a week later, in a field at Tealing, about six miles from the house where it had been removed.

This sounds more like a Whitehall farce than a story of the supernatural, but readers are assured it really did happen and has been well recorded in the Tealing parish records. How the corpse actually got from Monifieth to Tealing is as much a mystery today as it was over a century ago. The whole affair certainly had a marked effect on William Craighead. For the remainder of his life, he was never to play another practical joke – just the opposite in fact. He became far too serious and thoughtful and as he got older his mind began to go, until, just before his death, he had gone completely mad.

The Battle of Nechtanesmere, in which the Northumbrians under King Ecgfrith were decisively beaten by the Picts under Brude mac Beli, took place in May of AD 685. The Northumbrians, already in control of much of the Lothians, crossed the Firth at Stirling and the Tay at Perth, and then took a route through Strathmore, where the Picts were waiting for them at Dunnichen Hill. The Northumbrians were quickly put to flight, only to find themselves trapped between the charging Picts, and what was then the site of Nechtanes Mere. Ecgfrith and his royal bodyguard were slain, as was most of the Northumbrian army, and the few who managed to escape carried Ecgfrith's body with them, later giving it a royal burial at Iona.

Over twelve hundred years after the battle, in January 1950, Miss E.F. Smith, a professional woman in her late fifties, had been to a small dinner party at a friend's home in Brechin, ten miles to the north of her own home at Letham. It was late at night when she left and set off for home in her little car. There had been a fall of snow and, a few miles outside Brechin, her car skidded into a ditch. There was nothing that could be done and

Miss Smith had to abandon the vehicle and continue the remaining few miles of her journey on foot.

It was nearly two o'clock in the morning when Miss Smith, cold and tired, saw the lights of Letham village, which sits on a minor road between the present A958 and the A932. As she approached a crest in the road, beyond which lay Dunnichen Hill, she saw in the distance what seemed to be moving torches. As she got nearer the village, the flickering torches appeared to get nearer and she was able to make out groups of figures in the field to her right. They were no more than about fifty yards away, moving in the direction of some farm buildings.

She later estimated that the experience lasted no more than about ten minutes, ending as she left the scene behind her when she entered the village through which she then walked to her own home, a further quarter of a mile away. She never gave the torch-carrying figures another thought as, tired out after her long walk, she went straight to bed. It was only the following morning that she suddenly realized what a strange experience it had been. The more she thought about it, the stranger it seemed.

Discussing her experiences later, she said that what she had seen had not suddenly started as she approached, but that it had already been going on for a while when she arrived at the scene. She said that the figures quite near to her, which she could see plainly enough, appeared to be dressed in brown and wore dark tights the whole way up – a sort of overall with a roll collar, and at the bottom of the tunic there was a larger roll around them. She didn't see the feet, but she was sure none of the figures was wearing high boots. On their heads they wore a hard roll, 'the kind of thing baker's boys used to wear'.

Had she been witness to a replay of the aftermath of the Battle of Nechtanesmere? Certainly the activity of dealing with the dead after the battle would have continued well into the night and the following day. And Miss Smith's description of the torch-carrying figures does correspond with an incised picture of a Pictish warrior on a stone at Golspie, over one hundred miles away on the Durnoch Firth.

The Eilan Mor lighthouse stands on the rocky, isolated Flannan Islands, some twenty miles out in the Atlantic, off the Island of Lewis. On the night of 15 December 1900, as the lighthouse went dark, two seamen aboard the brigantine *Fair Wind* saw a strange sight. Cutting diagonally across their bow, a longboat with a huddle of men on board was bearing towards the lighthouse.

The sailors hailed the boat but there was no answer. They noted that the boatmen wore foul-weather gear and as the moonlight slashed through a break in the clouds their faces were illuminated. The sailors' first thoughts were that they were the floating dead from some shipwreck, but then they heard the oarlocks and saw the movement of their arms.

Later that night a squall blew up. Without the guardian light there was a real danger to shipping and the question several angry sea-captains were asking was: why was the lighthouse dark?

A few days later, the Trinity House vessel *Hesperus* hove to off the Flannan Islands to investigate. When there was no answer to repeated signals, crewmen set out in a small boat to the landing dock. As they were tying up the boat they were chilled by the strange, ominous silence. The lighthouse was, as is the rule, staffed by three keepers, but there was no one there to welcome the *Hesperus*. There were no signs of violence and the larders were well stocked. The lamps were all trimmed and ready, the beds made and the dishes and other kitchen utensils were shining in their racks.

As the searchers climbed through the empty lighthouse, they found only two things that struck them as unusual. On the stairway and in the tiny office, where the log was kept, there were shreds of a strange seaweed unknown to them. The other strange factor was that there were no oilskins or seaboots in the lighthouse, something which suggested that all three keepers had left together.

No lighthouse keeper has ever been known to abandon his post, even in the worst weather, and this point was repeatedly made during the inquiry which inevitably followed – an inquiry that was hushed to silence by the reading of the log kept by one of the keepers, Thomas Marshall:

> 'December 12: Gale N by NW Sea lashed to fury. Never seen such a storm. Waves very high. Tearing at Lighthouse. Everything shipshape. James Ducat irritable.'

And later that day:

> 'Storm still raging, wind steady. Stormbound. Cannot go out.

Ship passing and sounding foghorn. Could see cabin lights. Ducat quiet. Donald McArthur crying.'

'December 13: Storm continued through night. Wind shifted W. by N. Ducat quiet. McArthur praying.'

And another entry later in the day:

'Noon, grey daylight. Me, Ducat and McArthur praying.'

For some inexplicable reason, there was no entry for the 14 December. The final line in the log read: 'December 15, 1 p.m.: Storm ended, sea calm. God is over all.'

The only explanation the inquiry could put forward to account for the disappearance of the three lighthousekeepers, was that they had been hallucinating. For while the log entries had reported gales lashing the Flannan Isles, there had been none at all twenty miles away on the Island of Lewis!

Locals, however, point to an even more mysterious cause for the disappearance of the lighthousemen. For centuries the Flannan Islands have been haunted. The Hebridean farmers might sail there during daylight – and then only when they know there is a good chance of getting back before dusk – but few except the 'foolish sassenachs' at the lighthouse dared stay overnight. Final proof, if the locals needed it, was the evidence of the sailors of the *Fair Wind* – of the longboat crowded with ghosts.

February 1963 was the month of the great freeze-up. For three days a savage blizzard had been blowing, and the whole of Scotland was in the grip of an iron frost. At 3 a.m. on 8 February, almost blinded by the flurry of snowflakes whipped into his face by the ice-edged wind, a 35-year-old lorry driver battled his way along the bleak A74 which wound its way across the savage Beattock Summit.

About an hour before, his long-distance lorry had shuddered to a halt in a deep snowdrift, just one more to add to the scores of cars and lorries which had been abandoned by their drivers in the smothering 'white-out'. He had set off on foot for Beattock, the nearest village. Suddenly, the driver, Joe Turnbull, stopped dead in his tracks. A few yards in front of him in the moonlight, he saw a weird-looking hump, black against the glittering blanket of snow which covered the road. As he drew closer to it, the hump resolved itself into a sprawling human body. Joe dropped to his knees and began to claw at the snow around the partly-covered body. Gently he eased it over on its back, to discover it was that of a man in his mid-thirties who appeared to have been dead for some time.

Not really knowing what to do, Joe decided that, despite being frozen with the cold, he would have to carry the body to Beattock, about a mile-and-a-half away. He hoisted the man on to his shoulders and, staggering and stumbling in patches of knee-deep snow, began his hopeless journey. He managed to stagger about 300 yards before collapsing exhausted in the snow.

While pausing for breath before the next stage of his journey, Joe was relieved to hear voices and two figures emerged out of the swirling mist of snow. They were, like himself, long-distance lorry drivers, whose vehicles were snowbound. Joe showed them the body and explained the situation. They replied that they were themselves making for Beattock railway station, some distance from the village, and that they would take the body between them.

Joe watched as the two men carrying the corpse, one holding it by the shoulders and the other by the legs, disappeared into the swirling white desert and a mystery was born, for neither the drivers nor the dead body have ever been seen since!

As soon as he reached Beattock, Joe Turnbull reported his gruesome discovery to the police saying that he had found the body in the snow and had handed it over to two men in good faith. The police, after interviewing him, decided that he was sane and believed his story. A massive investigation on a par with a murder hunt was launched and extra police officers went out searching up and down the road, through the long line of stranded vehicles stuck in the snow. They even called in the dog-handlers. They traced every driver of every abandoned vehicle and accounted for everyone, but they found no trace of either the two men or the corpse.

They checked Joe's description of the dead man against that of every missing person on their files, but it fitted none of them. The police thought that once the weather improved and the snow melted they might find a clue, but they never did and no one has answered police appeals for information. Body and bearers appear to have vanished from the face of the earth. Nothing has been seen of them since and the file on the case still remains open.

An experience which has never been fully understood, has been recalled by Mrs Elizabeth Shipley of Hawick. She told me: 'In 1948, when I was five years old, I went to meet my father from work. I still don't understand what made me go and meet him. I saw him across the street at the same time as he saw me. He crossed the road and, taking my hand in his, we both walked together along the High Street. As we neared our close, my father stopped and turning to me he said: "You go home. I'll see you later." '

She said she went straight home and on reaching the flat told her mother where she had been and what her father had said. She continued: 'My mother became very angry and told me not to say such naughty things for my father had died a year earlier.'

Some minutes later there was a knock at the door and, when Mrs Shipley's mother answered it, she found a very distraught former workmate of her late husband standing outside. 'You'll never believe me,' he said 'but I just saw your Betty walking hand-in-hand along the street with Bob!'

She said: 'My mother calmed the man down and when he left she turned to me and said: "Betty, I'll never disbelieve you again." Then she sat down and sobbed.' Mrs Shipley said that she has never forgotten the experience and she still recalls the feeling of peace which came over her when she was holding her father's hand, although she still finds it impossible to explain.

Mr Jack Geddes of Aberdeen told me a similar unusual story of an experience he had in 1983 when, as a care assistant in a rehabilitation centre for alcoholics at Fyvie, he received a telephone call late one night, telling him that one of the residents had turned up at a house some two miles away.

With Mr N. Ogston, the warden, he went to collect the person and, on arrival at the house, discovered him sitting beside an electric fire, obviously very drunk. When he saw them, the man suddenly jumped and began speaking in a strange tongue which neither Mr Geddes nor Mr Ogston understood.

'Mr Ogston said that he must be possessed by an alcoholic evil spirit', Mr Geddes told me. 'Not knowing what to do I stood up and faced him, quoting as I did so a text from the Bible: "The blood of Christ cleanseth us all from sin." Immediately I saw a look of hatred come into the man's eyes and foam began to froth round his mouth.'

Mr Geddes said that the man glared at him for a moment and

then retorted: 'Stop looking at me with the eyes of Christ', before suddenly lunging at him and chasing him around the room. 'Not knowing quite what to do, I ran away from him,' he continued. 'Then I suddenly realized that this was a stupid thing to do, so I stopped and turned round to face my assailant, raising both hands in the air and saying: 'I command you evil spirit to come out of this man, in the name of Christ.' Then, instead of coming towards me, the man suddenly ran into the nearby kitchen.'

At the time, Mr Geddes was wearing a digital watch on his left wrist and, as he spoke the words of the text, his watch strap broke, one part of the strap falling to the ground and the watch flew through the air in a straight line for several feet towards the kitchen door, where it landed at the raving man's feet. In case he stood on it, Mr Geddes ran forward and picked up the watch which he put into his jacket pocket. Once they had calmed the man down, they returned to the rehabilitation centre where Mr Geddes was later able to examine his watch in more detail. It was obviously broken, as the face of it showed no sign of life.

He said: 'That weekend I went home to Aberdeen and whilst I was sitting quietly I thought to myself that if some spiritual force had wrenched the watch from my wrist, then a stronger force from God might be able to get it going again. You might think I'm crazy or something, but I put two fingers on the watch face and quoted to it several times the same text that had angered the alcoholic spirit. Believe it or not, the digital numbers slowly reappeared and the second numbers began to move again. Of course, it was the wrong time and date, but that was soon corrected.'

On the following Monday, Mr Geddes went to the local watchmaker's shop to buy a new strap. He said: 'The shop assistant looked at the missing strap and said: "It must have been wrenched off your wrist with some force. The spring is missing." I didn't tell her how it had happened or she would have thought me crazy.'

It is now over five years since the incident occurred and Mr Geddes tells me that the watch has been in perfect working order since, and is a perfect time-keeper. He has kept the broken strap just to remind him that such a thing did actually happen.

Anyone who is anyone in mountaineering circles will recognize the name of Sydney Scroggie. He is a highly popular and much respected mountaineer and one of those unique people one meets only once or twice in a lifetime. For Sydney is not only an excellent and knowledgeable climber, but he is also blind.

About twelve miles from Corrour, in the craggy but magnificent stretch of land between the shore of Loch Ericht and the Pass of Drumochter, there stands a tiny cottage, known locally as Benaldar Cottage, typical of many of the small cottages erected in the mountainous areas of Scotland to serve as a shelter for mountaineers, walkers and hunters. Looking more like a three-roomed hut than a conventional cottage it is said to be named after a butler who committed suicide there by hanging himself in one of the rooms, in the days when the Highlands were popular with Edwardian high society shooting parties.

Early in 1970, Sydney Scroggie along with a sighted companion spent one night in the cottage, tired out after a day in the mountains. The place was completely empty and devoid of any furnishings whatever, except for an ancient armchair and an equally ancient army camp bed. The two men stretched out on the floor in their sleeping bags and lay listening to the log fire crackling in the fireplace with the flames casting a warm flickering glow over the bare walls. Outside it was pitch dark and freezing cold, but the two climbers were snug and relaxed.

Suddenly, they heard what sounded like a scraping noise, as if someone was running their long fingernails down the door, the sort of noise that sets your teeth on edge. Then, a few minutes later, there came the thump of heavy boots, seemingly pacing the bare floorboards of the empty room next door. The footsteps continued pacing up and down for several minutes before stopping, leaving the air filled with an atmosphere of foreboding. Next there came a shuffling and bumping sound, as if someone was rearranging furniture in the next room, although both men knew it was empty. This noise continued for quite some time, developing finally into a long session of deep, loud groans.

There was no explanation. Both men knew the adjoining room was empty and besides, anyone going into it would have to pass Sydney and his companion as they lay on the floor. More was to come. On a ledge over the fireplace, the two men had placed their provisions which included an unopened box of biscuits. Suddenly, the box of biscuits rose into the air and sailed right across the room to land on the floor against the opposite wall – and not one biscuit was broken.

Then, for a grand finale, the door burst open, just as though someone had charged against it. There was an amazingly loud thump on the floor which was heavy enough to vibrate the floorboards.

When he was about fifteen years old, Andrew Warren lived with his grandfather near Loch Longavat on the Island of Lewis. His grandfather was an elder of the kirk and he was also an enthusiastic amateur geologist, filling his home with fossils from the pits and caves in the area. One morning he came home in a state of great excitement and made young Andrew go with him to look at some ancient remains he had discovered at the bottom of a deep tarn. Bending down, his grandfather pointed out the bones – a human skeleton with the head of a wolf!

Supposing it to be the head of some monstrosity, or even a practical joke, the boy said so and his grandfather exclaimed: 'It's a werewolf. This island was once overrun with them. Help me carry the remains to the house.'

The youngster did as his grandfather asked and they placed the remains on the kitchen table. That evening he was left alone in the house, grandfather having gone to a meeting of the kirk elders. For some time he amused himself by reading and then, thinking he heard a noise in the kitchen, Andrew went to investigate. There was no one about and being convinced it was only a rat that had disturbed him, he sat at the table alongside the remains of the alleged werewolf and waited to see if the noise would happen again.

He sat with his elbows on his knees looking at the floor and thinking of nothing in particular, when suddenly there was a loud rapping of knuckles on the window. Turning and looking up, he saw a dark face looking in at him, at first dim and indistinct. Then it became more and more complete until it developed into a perfectly defined wolf's head, terminating in the neck of a human being. Scared, Andrew still had enough common sense to look in every direction for a possible reflection, but there was no light either outside or inside, other than from the late evening sun.

This was no illusion, the face and features were unmistakably those of a wolf with its jaws distended, lips wreathed in a savage snarl, the teeth sharp and white, with light green eyes and pointed ears. The expression on the face was so malignant, the boy stared at it in horror. Then the 'thing' raised one hand, a slender hand like that of a woman with long, curved fingernails. Remembering what his grandfather had told him about evil spirits, Andrew crossed himself, but as this had no effect and he feared the 'thing' would get him, he rushed out of the kitchen and shut and locked the door firmly behind him. He spent the remainder of the time sitting and shaking with fright in the hall until his grandfather came home.

When he learned what had taken place, grandfather assured him that had he been there with his great faith in the Almighty, he would very soon have sent this force of evil packing. However, he did make the boy help him remove the bones from the kitchen and they returned to the tarn and re-interred them in the very spot where they had been discovered, and where, so far as I am aware, they remain to this day.

There is a similar story surrounding an old bothy near Falar in Glen Tilt, to the north of Blair Atholl.

This old bothy used to afford protection for the night for travellers and mountaineers, and when unoccupied it was very often used by poachers. Some sixty years ago, two poachers arrived at Falar on a bitterly cold night and gained entrance by smashing one of the windows. Once inside, they lit a fire but found there was no water to cook the salmon they had poached from the River Tilt. One of the men volunteered to go for some, but as the window was the only way out he had to climb out through it. He had just put one leg over the sill when he began to scream, calling to his companion that some 'fiend' had taken a firm hold of his leg and was tearing at it and sucking his blood.

There was a violent struggle and eventually the man managed to free himself, but he was terrified and in great pain. His friend dragged him back inside and, taking up his shotgun, he climbed out himself to search the ground, but he could find no trace of anyone or anything which might have attacked his partner. But in the distance, he could see what appeared to be white winged objects and faint blue lights which appeared to keep changing their position. Scared, he managed to obtain the water and hurried back as quickly as he could. Both men spent the remainder of the night in a state of terror.

The following morning they could find no trace of man or beast, their own footprints in the freshly fallen snow were all that were visible. I am told that the man bore the scars of his injury for the rest of his life and it was this incident which prevented the bothy from ever being used again. It is said, rather darkly by the local inhabitants, that the area has long had the reputation of being haunted by, of all things, a vampire and it is still given a wide berth even today.

One day, a man was crossing the hills between Loch Tuath and Loch Cuan with his dog, when he saw a tall woman with long yellow hair, standing and apparently watching his progress. At first he took her to be a real human being but, as he got closer to her, he suddenly realized that there was something not quite right about her. She seemed rather peculiar and shadowy.

When he first caught sight of the woman, his dog whined and began to show signs of fear but, as they got closer to her, it suddenly became angry and rushed at the figure, snarling and growling. The strange woman then snatched the animal up in her arms and ran off, disappearing behind a large rock. The man, although he was frightened, ran after the woman and on going behind the rock he found his dog lying dead in a pool of blood. Handfuls of hair had been torn out of its body and it appeared to have been strangled. Yet there was no sign of the woman, nor was there anywhere nearby where she could have hidden.

Similarly, something strange and animal-like is said to haunt Hynish Hill on the south-west of the island of Tiree. According to tradition, it is something 'naked, not unlike a human body in form, but with a grotesque and diabolical wolf-like face'. This spectre is said to have been seen occasionally in broad daylight, though more often in the early hours of the morning. Its main characteristic again seems to be an intense dislike of dogs.

Locals tell of how one day, a dog belonging to a Tiree fisherman was found on the beach with its skin completely scraped off as if by long nails or claws. It was terribly mutilated and died in great pain shortly after it was discovered.

If you take the B869, from Stoer to Lochinver, you will encounter the gloomy Creag an Ordain, a huge rocky overhang above the road. Even today this is a very eerie spot to stop off and, according to tradition, it has long been haunted by a huge ghostly black dog. Normally, this apparition makes itself visible to walkers but, nowadays, with more and more cars on the road, he seems to have been scared off as he is hardly ever seen anymore. But since then, a mysterious light is frequently seen hovering over the area, which has so far remained unexplained.

One night earlier this century, a man was walking along the B869 on his way to the village of Clachtoll, when he heard splashing coming from the waters of Loch Ordain, which runs alongside the road. By the light of the moon, he saw a large black dog 'with eyes like glowing peat' emerge from the loch and scramble straight up the steep embankment towards him. He was terrified, to say the least, as the animal growled and 'spat sparks' at him.

Gathering what strength he could muster, the man suddenly turned and fled in terror along the road, the dog following him all the way. Gradually it overtook him and then, stopping in its tracks, it turned round to look at him. The man said he saw a hideous face, part human in form, with horns or antlers sticking out of its head.

As he continued on his way, the dog trotted in front of him, periodically looking back and growling, snarling and 'belching fire' from its grotesque mouth, until all of a sudden it disappeared from the centre of the road, giving a peal of horrific laughter as it did so. It is recorded that for a long time afterwards the man was quite seriously ill as a result of his encounter with the foul creature.

There are numerous reports of spectral dogs throughout the Highlands and islands and several old Highlanders claim to have often seen one following them in some of the more remote glens. They say that often, these dogs will bark once or twice and most sincerely believe that so long as the dog barks no more than twice, then they are quite safe; but three barks are a sure sign that the animal will overtake them, in which case they, or someone quite close to them, will be dead within a very short time.

The A87, from Loch Cluanie to Loch Duich, is a comparatively modern road running through Glen Shiel. About fifty years ago the old road through here was quite a hazardous drive for motorists, being so narrow that when another car was sighted travelling in the opposite direction, it was necessary to draw in at one of the passing places or lay-bys to allow the other vehicle to pass.

Just before the Second World War, a number of drivers reported identical experiences on the old Glen Shiel road. They would see a car travelling towards them in the far distance which almost immediately disappeared round a bend in the road. Since the road was so twisting, there was nothing at all peculiar about this, and the well-mannered driver would immediately look for a passing-place and pull into it to await the oncoming vehicle. But it never arrived. It mysteriously failed to materialize, nor did anyone ever come across it on resuming their journey.

All this took place on an isolated road, with no turn-offs or farm tracks which might have concealed another vehicle. At night, the spectral car took on the form of oncoming headlights which would similarly vanish behind a bend, never to reappear. Too many people – including a professor from Glasgow University, who saw the phantom twice – have witnessed it for it to be dismissed simply as a fancy. What makes this case all the more baffling, is that there does not seem to be any local tradition, such as a fatal accident, which would even attach a supernatural logic to the phenomenon. Despite the new road, the phantom motor car of Glen Shiel remains as puzzling today as it did fifty years ago.

# 8   Green Jean
# and the Dark Gentlemen

Just as we in England have our 'White Ladies', Scotland claims
its fair share of female phantoms in the form of 'Green Jean'. I
have been unable to discover just where the name came from,
but I think it possibly derives from the Gaelic, as most – though
by no means all – stories of Green Jean appear to have their
origins in the Highlands in the isolated old castles, manor
houses and lonely glens. There are still many unspoilt places in
the more remote districts of the Highlands where strange things
shrouded in mystery do still occur even in this day and age.

One of the best known ghosts of Ashintully Castle, on the A924
between Pitlochry and Blairgowrie, is that of 'Green Jean'.

According to tradition the castle and its surrounding lands
were once occupied by a girl named Jean whose uncle, jealous of
her wealth and position, made plans to murder her and inherit
the estate. One evening, while her maid was combing out her
hair, the uncle entered her bedchamber and cut her throat. It so
happened that she was wearing a green dress which was
considered at that time to be an unlucky colour.

To prevent the crime being discovered, the uncle was obliged
to murder the maid too, disposing of her body by stuffing it up
the chimney, before he dragged the body of Jean downstairs. To
this day her muffled footsteps are heard roaming the
passageways of Ashintully Castle – and the chimney where the
maid's body was hidden is said never to have drawn properly
since.

The small walled private burial ground attached to the castle
is reputedly the spot to visit if one wishes to catch sight of Green
Jean, who can often be seen standing at the headstone which

her uncle erected to her memory, in what is one of the weirdest places I have ever had occasion to visit.

At Blairgowrie, on the A923, fourteen miles north-west of Dundee, stands Newton Castle, said to have been built in the fourteenth century. It was ransacked by Cromwell and by the Duke of Montrose, and in 1745 was occupied by forces under the Duke of Cumberland.

According to an old ballad it is haunted by 'The Ladye Jean', the ghost of a lady in a green dress. Jean was in love with a young local chieftain who jilted her. She resolved to win him back and decked herself out in silks and satins and silver buckled shoes. She braided her raven hair and entwined it with pearls and jewels to match the fairness of her skin. Yet despite her efforts her lover remained unmoved, and night after night she sat in one of the castle towers, singing plaintive love songs until daybreak.

One day she consulted a local witch and she was told that the only way she could win back her lover was to dress herself in the 'cloth of the fairies'. She was instructed to cut a swathe of grass from the churchyard and a branch from a rowan tree on the gallows hill and tie her offering with a plaited reed. She was then to take it at dusk to the Corbie Stone where she was to sit down.

Jean made her way at dusk to the Corbie Stone with her offering and sat down closing her eyes. At first she heard only the sighing of the wind through the trees, but then an owl hooted. Suddenly she heard the sound of tinkling laughter and a chill wind blew around her, seemingly pulling at her dress. She sat with closed eyes while the fairy weavers worked until the dawn arrived. When she opened her eyes she saw she was decked out from head to toe in 'the witchin claith o'green'.

Meanwhile back at Newton Castle, Lord Ronald waited for his bride, for she was to marry him despite her love for another man. Soon she returned and sadly took her place beside him still clad in her strange green gown. The marriage took place but afterwards, when Sir Ronald looked down at his lovely bride, he saw that she was distraught and he felt her hand which was ice-cold. Then she gave an unearthly cry and died in his arms.

She was buried at Knockie Hill where her grave can still be found today, with a stone set at the head. People say that even nowadays, on All-Hallows Eve, when the midnight bell rings from the church, the stone is seen to revolve three times before Green Jean rises from her grave and drifts off towards Newton Castle.

At Castle Grant in Morayshire they possess a small, quite ordinary looking bedroom in the old tower, which is reached by a stone staircase, thickly carpeted in tartan. This pleasant little room is hung with tapestries said to have been woven by twenty ladies who once lived there in exile.

Regularly, the figure of a woman is said to appear through the tapestry hangings on the wall: a small woman, in no way frightening, who goes through the motions of appearing to wash her hands. She then darts across the room to disappear through a door leading to a winding staircase. No one knows who she is, but many people say she is probably the ghost of Barbara Grant, the daughter of a sixteenth-century laird.

Opening off the bedroom there is a dark closet and local legend is that Barbara was imprisoned there by her father for refusing to marry the man he had chosen for her. It is said that rather than yield to her father's wishes and marry a man who was both ugly and cruel, she preferred to remain and die in her dark cupboard.

According to tradition the ruined mansion at Woodhouselee is haunted by another Green Jean, actually a woman in white, said to be the shade of Lady Hamilton of Bothwellhaugh.

This poor woman, together with her baby was, during the absence of her husband, stripped naked and turned out of doors on a bitterly cold January night, by a favourite of the Regent Murray. Why he did this one can only surmise, but as a result of his inhuman conduct the baby died, and its mother with the baby's corpse in her arms, was discovered the following morning, raving mad.

When her husband returned she had to be locked away for her own safety and since her death, her white-clothed ghost has been seen on numerous occasions, drifting through the ruins apparently searching for her baby.

A white lady haunts the grounds of Rownam Manor, near Stirling. This spectre is thought to be that of a former lady of the manor whose death, at an early age, was said to have been hastened, if not entirely accounted for, by her husband's harsh treatment. Whether the husband was as black as he was painted is a matter of conjecture, but the intense animosity with which people remember him, made the local populace ready to attribute all the alleged hauntings by this particular Green Jean to his past misdeeds.

Today she is said to roam the grounds, a glowing figure draped in a quantity of white drapery, thought to be a winding sheet. Streaming over her neck and shoulders are thick masses of long, wavy golden hair and her face, despite its pallor, is said to be so beautiful as to be unforgettable.

Often she is seen in the company of a man, thought to be the shade of her former husband, whose attitude obviously changed in the after-life for he walks with one arm around her trim waist and his whole body is illuminated by the light coming from her body.

There is a house on the shores of Loch Ness which, when built at the end of the sixteenth century, must have been a fine residence indeed.

On the night before the Battle of Culloden, a number of Highland chieftains were discussing their plans in one of the large rooms of the house. Their talk, of course, was secret, but during the course of it one of the chiefs heard a slight sound of movement behind a wooden panel. On investigating, the young daughter of the house was discovered, apparently spying on them. She was dragged out screaming and put to death on the spot.

Over the years, members of the household and several guests have been wakened at night by the most blood-curdling female screams. The sound is said to be something tragic and inexpressibly distressing, which upsets all those who hear it.

Early last century, Skibo Castle in Easter Ross was left in charge of the steward who induced a flighty local girl to visit him there. One night she failed to return home and it was widely believed that she had been murdered. However, despite intensive searches and enquiries, nothing could be found which might incriminate the man.

A few years later he left his position and went to live abroad. It was after this that the hauntings began, and they were to continue for many years. The corridors often echoed to unearthly screams and the apparition of a terrified partly-clothed woman would go flitting through the house. It was only when the castle was bought by Andrew Carnegie, and repairs and alterations were being carried out, that the bones of a woman were found embedded in a wall. Once the remains had been given a decent Christian burial, the hauntings ceased.

An Tigh Mor, or The Big House, is now derelict. At one time it was the home of the MacDonalds, and here on dark nights the whole of the west wing of the empty building is seen to be brilliantly lit. Those who dare to investigate – and these are few and far between – have reported hearing doors opening and shutting, although no other human beings have been around.

At other times, a woman in white has been seen passing from the east to the west wing, from where she then drifts up to the attics. Although many people give differing versions as to her identity, it still remains a complete mystery to this day.

A mile or so south of Loch Glassie, just off the B846 between Aberfeldy and Pitcastle, you will find Tom Buidhe, a well-known haunted farmhouse.

Many years ago, a servant girl from a nearby farm had fallen in love with the son of the now haunted house. He on the other hand, was in love with someone else and married a girl in his own social class. On the day of the wedding, the rejected servant girl drowned herself in a water butt outside the house and, that same night, her ghost put the fear of God into the newly-weds by appearing in the bridal chamber sobbing and wringing her hands. The young farmer tried to cast the apparition from his mind, but his bride of only a few hours went insane and within a week she was dead.

Not so many years ago, a tourist stayed at the farm, and one night, lying awake in bed, he heard the sound of a woman crying. As he listened, the crying grew louder and seemed to approach the bed. Then he saw, silhouetted against the moonlight, the face of a pretty young girl, which evolved into a tall woman in a white dress. Her eyes were big dark and beautiful although full of sorrow, and she appeared to be wringing her hands in despair.

The man was not in the least frightened and he asked the figure what the matter was. But she didn't answer, she just stood looking at him for several seconds before sinking to the floor, sobbing. She looked so real that the man got out of bed to try to comfort her but, when he turned on the light, his ghostly visitor had disappeared. Not a trace of her could be found in the room, although for some time afterwards he could still hear the distinct sound of her sobbing.

Ruthven Castle, mentioned elsewhere in this book, had a Green Jean, or in this case 'Lady Greensleeves' who acted as an augurer of the future, particularly of approaching death.

One stormy night a traveller came to Ruthven Castle seeking shelter. The owner was away, but the steward took him in and offered him a fine large bedroom in which a lovely log fire was burning. Because of the noise of the storm outside, the stranger was unable to sleep. As he lay tossing and turning, he heard the clock strike midnight and as it did so, a tall woman dressed in green suddenly appeared in the room. Her face was full of grief as she leant over the bed and looked at the man who, terror-stricken, called out: 'In the name of God. Who are you madam?'

There was no answer, and when the fire suddenly blazed up in the hearth, he realized that the green lady had vanished, but had left traces of her tears on the pillow beside him. His terrified shouts brought the steward running to his room and the two men spent the remainder of the night sitting by the fire.

Early the next morning, the traveller left to continue his journey to Perth, and a few days later it was learned that he had been drowned crossing the River Tay. The steward remained convinced right up until his own death several years later, that Lady Greensleeves had come to warn the traveller of his impending death.

Some strange things were said to have taken place at an old house at Ardgay, on the A9 a few miles south of Bonar Bridge.

One night, the old lady who lived there was startled when her kettle was lifted right off the hob by unseen hands, following which she heard pots and pans being thrown about in the scullery. She was so afraid that she ran screaming from the house and went round to the church to obtain the protection of the minister.

A no-nonsense pragmatist, the minister gathered up his Bible and set off to the house to deal with the 'evil that has fallen upon it'. When he arrived he was immediately bombarded with turnips and potatoes which appeared from nowhere. But, Bible in hand he refused to be intimidated and volunteered to spend the night there.

The old lady put him up in her spare bedroom and the minister settled down for a night's sleep, but at around midnight his room door burst open. The minister realized he had left his Bible downstairs, so he went down and retrieved it and then bolted his bedroom door again. Then he saw, reflected in the dressing-table mirror, the figure of a large woman dressed in black, yet when he turned round to face her she had completely vanished. Nevertheless he could hear footsteps approaching nearer and nearer to where he stood clutching his Bible.

Then all went quiet and he laid his Bible on the bed and offered up a prayer, asking the spirit to depart for good. By all accounts it did so and there was no further trouble. Afterwards, the minister made some enquiries and discovered that many years before, a maid-servant employed at the house had given birth to an illegitimate child. She had suffocated it and had hidden its little body in the drawer of the dressing table in that same room.

In May, 1875, three sisters went to live at Glen Mallan, which stands alongside Loch Long on the A814 in Dunbartonshire (now Strathclyde), where their parents had taken a house which had belonged to a gardener and his wife.

One day, two of the sisters had gone to the village leaving the youngest, Lucy, alone in the house. When they returned, they met Lucy running down the road towards them in a real state of agitation. She told them that an old woman had taken up residence in the kitchen, and was lying on the bed with her clothes and boots on. She said she thought the old woman was a tinker body – a gypsy – and she was afraid to go back into the house alone.

The sisters hurried back to the house and Lucy, entering the kitchen first, cried: 'Look. There she is!' and pointed to the bed. The older sisters looked, but all they saw was a flat and unruffled bed. Lucy persisted and when she was satisfied her sisters saw no woman, she became so frightened she turned hysterical and had to be taken out of the room and calmed down.

Two days later, the whole family were sitting around the kitchen fire, when the youngest daughter suddenly sat upright and said: 'There is the old woman again, lying the same way!' This time there were no hysterics and she was able to describe what she saw: an old woman lying on top of the bedcovers, with her clothes and boots on, and with her knees drawn up as if she was cold. Her face was to the wall and she wore a 'sow-backed mutch' – a sort of mob-cap – frilled at the front and sticking out at the back, a drab petticoat and a checked shawl drawn tight round her shoulders. The girl said she could not see the old woman's face, but her right hand, yellow, thin and wrinkled like that of a hard working countrywoman, was hugging her left arm.

The girl continued to see the figure, but the remainder of the family could see nothing and referred to it jokingly as 'Lucy's old woman'.

As the summer wore on, the family began to get to know their neighbour and one day during a discussion with her, the sisters brought up the subject of the strange apparition allegedly seen by Lucy. At the girl's description, the neighbour nearly fainted, saying that it sounded just like the first wife of the man who had lived at the house before they moved in.

Malcolm and Kate had lived conflicting lives, she being a hard-working woman, while he was a man who preferred to spend his time drinking in the village inn. One day they went to market and he bought a half gallon of whisky, which after a time, and apparently after helping himself, he gave to his poor wife to carry. Kate went on ahead with it and was back at the house first. When Malcolm arrived home, he accused her of having drunk some of it, and he gave her such a severe beating that he was afraid he might have seriously harmed her.

He went to the neighbour's house and told her his wife was ill and, when she visited the house, she found Kate lying on the bed, just as Lucy had described. She had her face to the wall to hide the result of her husband's brutal beating. Kate later died of her appalling injuries.

For every female spectre in Scotland there is a male counterpart – a 'Black Jamie' perhaps? Although in many cases they might not be as romantic as their female companion, these ghosts are nevertheless equally interesting.

Should you drive along the B9006, from Cray to Inverness, just before reaching the battle site at Culloden Moor you will pass the site of the old railway station. Between here and the battleground will be found Culloden House, known locally as 'The Castle'. At one time the house contained a large number of relics, such as the bed in which Bonnie Prince Charlie is supposed to have slept on the night before the battle. (How many beds are there in Scotland where Bonnie Prince Charlie is said to have slept? Had he slept in every one which claims this honour, he would hardly have found the time to fight the English.) There was also his walking stick and several swords, pistols and battle-axes, all said to have been picked up from time to time on the battlefield. The house is also said to contain a ghost, thought to be that of Bonnie Prince Charlie himself.

Some years ago the house was open to the public during the summer season. Returning from Inverness one evening, well after the last visitor should have left, the proprietress was surprised to see a tall figure clad in tartan, with a plaid of grey walking along a corridor and entering a room at the far end. Knowing that there was no way out of the house through this room, she hurried after the man to ask what he was doing, only to find the room empty.

A woman relative once saw the figure, in dark clothing, cross an upstairs landing. As the rooms on that floor were not in use at the time she felt quite alarmed, particularly when no further trace of the man could be found. It is alleged that this same figure has been seen on a number of other occasions since, and no one seems to doubt for one minute that this is the ghost of Charles Edward Stuart.

If, by any chance, you should be strolling along some isolated Highland seashore and stumble across some personal belongings, especially if these belongings are those of a sailor and have been washed ashore from some shipwreck, you would be well advised to take heed of the following story and leave them where they lie for, should you be tempted to pick them up, the chances are that the ghost of the former owner will come and ask for them back.

One day at Sheigra, a small community at the end of the B801, north-west of Kinlochbervie, a crofter picked up the belongings of a sailor who drowned off the coast nearby. Some nights later, a strange man suddenly materialized in his croft. He was dressed in the clothes of a sea-farer and after walking about the room for some time, he just as mysteriously disappeared again. For several nights afterwards the ghostly sailor appeared, each time staying a little longer, until in time he began to get violent and started throwing the furniture about.

The crofter, who was by now frightened, summoned the local minister who advised him that he should confront the ghost boldly and ask what it was he wanted. Eventually the crofter picked up enough courage and spoke to the ghost who replied in Gaelic. No one knows what was said, but following this the crofter and the spectre walked out of the croft together and went down to the shore, where the ghostly seaman walked straight out in the water and slowly dissolved into nothingness.

All the whisky in Scotland could not induce the crofter to reveal the conversation that had passed between them, but by all accounts the ghostly seaman has never been seen since.

Avock stands on the A832 alongside Inverness Firth, about three miles from Fortrose. It is a delightful little spot on the Black Isle, that finger of land which is surrounded by the Cromarty Firth to the north and Moray Firth to the east.

About sixty years ago there was a house there which was rented for the summer by a Lowland businessman and his family. It had stood empty for almost a year and when the house agent was showing them around, he advised against using a certain bedroom, murmuring something about 'the noise'. Despite the warning, when the family settled in, this particular bedroom was allocated to their young son.

A week later the boy complained that some of his things had been tampered with and that he had heard footsteps in his room in the dark. He was sure that his older brothers were playing tricks on him, so one night he took his dog to bed with him, thinking that he would be sure to bark if anyone came into the room. After he had been asleep for some time, he was wakened by the growling of the dog, and, sitting up in bed, the boy was astonished to see a faint glowing outline of a boy of about his own age, crossing from the door to the window. The snarling dog stood staring at the ghostly intruder, its fur standing on end.

The boy called out in alarm and his father and elder brothers came running. Hearing his story, they searched the house and garden, but there was no sign of any intruder. It was later learnt that a few years before, whilst walking in his sleep, the only son of the owner of the house had been killed by falling out of the bedroom window and that his ghost was believed to haunt the house.

An Edinburgh lady was invited to stay with her friend at Ardnadam, on the A815 a few miles north of Dunoon.

At breakfast on her first morning there, she asked her hostess who the old gentleman was who was also staying with her. The hostess was surprised and said there was no one else staying at the house. The woman then went on to explain how she was coming downstairs to breakfast when she met an old gentleman in a white silk shirt and trousers, with a red-coloured sash around his waist and a red turban on his head. He had stood to one side to let her pass and as she did so, he gave a polite bow. Then she saw his face, which was leathery and wrinkled, as if he had spent most of his life in a hot climate.

The lady enjoyed her holiday. No more was seen of the strange man and when she left to return home the incident was forgotten. Then, several months later, the son of the house came to stay with his mother. She put him up in a bedroom at the back of the house, above which was an attic room, used to store the usual household junk. One morning at breakfast he said to his mother: 'What were you doing, dragging furniture about in the middle of the night?' His mother was surprised, she had slept right through the night without once being disturbed.

Her son explained that he had heard someone in the room above him, seemingly dragging furniture over to the door. He heard drawers being opened, following which there was a loud bang, as if someone had fired a pistol. Mother and son checked the attic room and found everything in order and were unable to find anything which could possibly explain the noises.

Intrigued, the son decided to research into the history of the house and he discovered that some years before his mother had moved in, it had been occupied by a retired army colonel who had served for many years in India. He had moved to Ardnadam, on being discharged from the army, where he soon established a reputation for dressing in an eccentric fashion. One morning, his servants had heard a pistol shot and after

rushing up to the attic they found they were unable to open the
door. The colonel had piled furniture against it and, when the
servants managed to push it open, the old man was found dead
on the floor with his smoking revolver lying close by.

Auchindoune is a square, comfortable-looking mansion with an
excellent view, well cared for gardens and tastefully furnished
rooms. It stands on part of the Cawdor Castle estate, about five
miles from Culloden. Built about 1700, the house was once
tenanted by a certain Hamish Munroe who, after the Battle of
Culloden, gave shelter to a party of Jacobites escaping from the
carnage.

Munroe hid them in the extensive cellars at Auchindoune, but
a party of Cumberland's men came looking for them.
Subsequently the refugees and Munroe were taken out into the
gardens, stood against a wall and shot.

In later years the house was occupied by Dr Hector Munroe
who lived there alone. One day, having returned from a
strenuous hunt, he was relaxing and reading in front of the
drawing-room fire when he realized the room had suddenly
become extremely cold. There was a good fire blazing in the
hearth, yet he was shivering. Then, he looked up and saw that a
mist had formed by the mantelpiece and, as he watched, it
formed itself into an evil-looking human face which suddenly
spoke to him and said: 'Get out!' Dr Munroe felt urged to leave
the room as quickly as possible, and when he got outside into
the passage he realised that here it was quite warm, despite the
fact that it was a cold winter's night, compared with the
drawing-room and its blazing fire.

Some years later, his daughter-in-law was sitting alone in the
drawing-room with her two dogs, who suddenly began to whine
and become extremely agitated. She tried to calm them, but they
continued to whine and snarl, looking beyond her to the back of
the room. Then they began to crawl backwards, apparently
terrified at something they alone could see, until they were
almost under her chair. The room became very cold and the
woman sensed an indescribably evil presence. Overcome by
fear, she made the sign of the cross and walked quickly to the
door, followed by the cowering, snarling dogs.

The place where the Redcoats shot the Jacobite refugees can
still be seen; the pockmarks on the kitchen garden wall being

the only evidence of the atrocity which took place there. Today, many local inhabitants swear that, around the anniversary of the Battle of Culloden, the swirl of pipes and the tramp of marching Highlanders can be heard in the neighbourhood.

There are other ghosts at Auchindoune. Again in the drawing-room the rustle of silk like the swish of a woman's dress has sometimes been heard crossing the room, and in the garden, the ghost of a brown-haired, bare-footed young woman, wearing a faded blue print frock, has often been seen gathering wild flowers. She is thought to be the ghost of Elspeth Munroe, the daughter of Hamish, who, in the latter years of the eighteenth century eloped with an under-shepherd who worked on the Cawdor Castle estate.

And finally, a story which, like those of the phantom hitch-hiker, has several different variations throughout the length and breadth of Britain. This particular story was told to me by Mr James Duggan, a former porter who had worked much of his life at Glasgow Central Station. He claims he knew the man to whom the story relates.

James McLeary was making his way to Glasgow Central Station on a foggy winter's night early this century. As he made his way from the Western Infirmary, where he was a junior houseman, the fog came down thicker, so that by the time he had reached the junction of Sauchiehall Street and Argyll Street, he was groping about in fog so thick that he lost his way.

Suddenly, a voice came out of the gloom beside him: 'Have you lost your way, sir? Follow me.' McLeary said that he wanted to get to Central Station, to which the voice replied that he was going there too and McLeary should follow him. McLeary, who had only been in the city for a short time, didn't need any second bidding and, as the man's voice sounded pleasant and well-educated, he thought he may have been a member of the University staff or from the hospital, and he stuck to him like glue.

So thick was the fog, even the trams were not running. Indeed, no traffic noises could be heard in the usually busy street. The only sound was of their own footsteps which echoed hollowly in what McLeary hoped was Argyll Street. The air was damp and cold and twice they passed coughing figures, struggling like themselves to find their destination in the curling yellow pea-soup of the fog. McLeary was relieved when he found himself in the comparatively well-lit station forecourt. He turned and thanked the stranger for his assistance and they walked together into the nearly deserted station entrance.

'Are you catching the Carlisle train?' the stranger asked. When McLeary told him he was, but only as far as Motherwell, the stranger, to his delight, told him that he too was catching the same train and suggested they share a compartment together.

They got into an empty second class compartment and noticed that the fog was now beginning to thin a little. As the train pulled out of Glasgow Central, the stranger said: 'The weather is similar now, to what it was on this night two years ago.'

McLeary, surprised, asked him how he could remember such a particular night after so long. 'I have good reason to,' the stranger answered. He then went on to explain how he had boarded the train at Glasgow Central, just as they had done and, as it began to pull out from the platform, he was congratulating himself on having got a compartment to himself. Suddenly, with the train beginning to gather speed, the door opened and a man jumped in. 'He sat opposite me and I did not like the look of him one little bit.'

The stranger went on to say that the man had a low, sloping forehead, a long nose, piercing eyes and wore a greasy cap and a dirty ill-fitting suit. He looked as if he might have been a shipyard worker or a heavy manual labourer.

'At the time I was a merchant in Glasgow with a substantial business in Argyll Street, and in my valise, which was by my side, I had nearly £200, the day's takings. I vaguely noticed the man glancing at the valise, and as I was tired, coupled with the motion of the train, I felt quite sleepy. In fact, I was just dropping off when a movement from the man opposite roused me. He was holding a knife in his hand and before I could take any action to defend myself, he jumped on me and a violent struggle took place.'

McLeary said: 'You were obviously the winner.'

'No,' replied the stranger. 'My assailant was very strong and much younger than me. I tried to get at the communication cord, but he drew me back and plunged his knife into my chest.'

'But obviously he missed any vital organs,' said McLeary with obvious interest. 'You were very fortunate.'

'No,' the stranger said. 'He plunged it into my heart and killed me!'

McLeary gasped, looking up and not believing his ears. There was no reply. The stranger had vanished. McLeary was alone in the compartment and the train was rattling along at over fifty miles an hour, approaching the outskirts of Motherwell!

Imagination? A tall story? Perhaps. But records show that in February, 1911, one Joseph Patrick Noon, a 27-year-old married warehouse worker from Govan, was executed at Glasgow's Barlinnie Prison, after being found guilty of murdering businessman George Ferguson on the Glasgow/Euston train. Mr Ferguson's body was discovered when the train stopped at Motherwell. Robbery had been the motive.

# 9 Weird Sisters

No book on Scottish ghosts and legends would be complete without at least a mention of some of the more infamous witches who spread fear and terror throughout the nation, particularly during the seventeenth century, when the witch-mania was at its height.

Witchcraft did not become a capital offence in Britain until 1563. Even then, English law required proof of injury to people or domestic animals but, in Scotland, a so-called 'pact' with the Devil was sufficient to incur the death penalty. In England only about half a dozen people were burned for witchcraft and about 1,000 hanged whereas, by comparison, in Scotland between 1563 and 1736, more than 4,400 witches died at the stake.

The Scots' fear of witchcraft was closely allied to the rise of the Reformed Church, though people believed in witches long before the Reformation. The new Protestants denounced the Catholic candles, bells and holy water as Papist superstitions, saying that if a man was steadfast in God, neither the Devil nor his agents could injure his immortal soul. This was of little comfort to people who believed the Devil stood constantly by their side, and that a witch's curse could kill or maim their animals or themselves. Medicine was only in its infancy, so a sudden illness – particularly a stroke or heart-attack – was easily seen as the result of witchcraft.

After about 1600, the number of witch prosecutions rose sharply throughout Britain, mainly due to the increasing influence of the uncompromising Protestant sects and their interpretation of Exodus XXII verse 18: 'Thou shalt not suffer a witch to live.' So in Scotland, at least, a supposed witch could be brought to trial by any anonymous, unsupported accusation, and it would have been extremely difficult for the accused to prove her innocence. Evidence was twisted and corrupted to suit the prosecution and the sentence was invariably one of death.

This does not, however, mean that all witches were innocent of at least attempting the crime with which they were charged. Both the courts and the accused believed strongly in the reality of witchcraft, and many witches were convinced of their own powers, often basking in the notoriety this brought them.

In 1590, a group of women stood on the pier at Leith, staring out to sea. One of them held a struggling black cat which had pieces of human flesh, taken from a hanged man, tied to its paws. Suddenly, the woman flung the screeching animal into the cold waters of the Firth of Forth. Instantly, clouds gathered, the wind began to howl and the sea rose and pounded against the shore. A sudden squall hit a boat sailing across the Firth and it heeled over drunkenly, before sinking with all hands.

The women were the notorious witches of North Berwick and their macabre ceremony was an attempt to raise a storm and sink the ship in which King James VI and his new bride, Anne of Denmark, were returning home from Norway. Fortunately the boat which foundered was not the right vessel, and the royal ship managed to reach port safely.

This unlikely story first came to light when the deputy bailiff of Tranent, David Seaton, noticed that his maid, Gilly Duncan, was behaving oddly. She kept leaving the house at night without his permission, and had aquired something of a reputation as a healer and wise-woman. With suspicions of witchcraft dawning, Seaton questioned her and, when she refused to answer, he tortured her. But still she kept her silence. During the interrogation, when a mole was found on the unfortunate maid's throat, it was supposed that she was the Devil's agent, and it therefore proved her identity as a witch. Under further torture, she admitted that her cures were inspired by the Devil, and that she belonged to a witch coven, the members of which she was forced to expose.

From her confessions there emerged details of a plot to kill King James. The instigator was said to be the Earl of Bothwell, the king's cousin and heir presumptive if James should die with- out issue. Bothwell was said to be the leader of the coven and presided over its meetings wearing a ritual disguise. Despite her giving several names, only four people were brought to trial: John Fian, Euphemia MacLean, Barbara Napier and Agnes Simpson, a local midwife whose herbal remedies were well known in the district.

Under torture, John Fian confessed that he was 'clerk to all those that were in subjection to the Devil's service'. In other words, he kept a list of names of members of the coven and administered their oaths. He said that at their meetings, he always stood at the Devil's left elbow. Later Fian retracted his confession and despite further torture he remained silent. He was found guilty however and was strangled and burnt at Edinburgh in January 1591.

Agnes Simpson was examined by King James himself at Holyrood House. She told him that after failing to sink his ship, she begged one of his courtiers to give her a piece of old linen once worn by the king. The courtier refused, otherwise she would have smeared it with toad's venom and James would have died in agony. She also revealed that the witches had gathered one night at Prestonpans, where they chanted curses over a wax image of King James, passing it from hand to hand as they chanted: 'This is King James VI, ordained to be consumed at the instance of a noble man, Francis Hepburn, Earl of Bothwell.'

The king heard Agnes and the other witches give accounts of a great assembly of witches at North Berwick church on All-Hallows Eve, 1590, their use of the church being a matter of convenience, rather than deliberate blasphemy. According to Agnes, two hundred witches were there. They went by sea, making merry on the way with flagons of wine. At the churchyard, Gilly Duncan provided the music on a Jew's harp as the throng danced round, singing as they did so. She said that the Devil presided over the gathering, in the form of a man wearing a black gown and mask. She said his hands were hairy and had claws on them, and his feet had talons! All paid homage to him and then he stood in the pulpit, with black candles burning all around. Here he preached to his followers concerning the obedience they owed him, urging them to work evil on his greatest enemy, King James VI.

King James, who had been following the evidence with great attention, suddenly lost his patience and stood up, calling the witches extreme liars. A rather unusual action for James, who was a deeply superstitious man. Then Agnes did an incredible thing; she said she would tell him something he would not doubt. Drawing the king to one side, she whispered to him the words that had passed between Anne of Denmark and himself on their wedding night.

Shaken, the king was now convinced that Agnes was telling the truth, but it also signed her death warrant. He knew that she could not have learned what she had just told him by mortal means, and so she was convicted of witchcraft. Agnes, along with Euphemia MacLean and Gillie Duncan, was executed on Edinburgh's Castle Hill. Barbara Napier was released and Bothwell, the prime mover in the case, fled to Naples where he was said to have practiced sorcery until he died in poverty in 1624.

In 1705, three people died and many others suffered cruel tortures, as a result of a number of wild accusations of witchcraft made by a 16-year-old boy, Patrick Morton, of Pittenween, a small seaside town on the A917 between Anstruther and St Monance in Fife.

One of those who died was Beatrix Laing, wife of a former town councillor, who stood accused of sending evil spirits to torment Patrick. After five months alone in a lightless and airless dungeon, and frequent visits to the torture chamber, she was freed, only to die a short time later, friendless and broken. Another of the accused, Thomas Brown, was starved to death in his dungeon and a third, Janet Bornfoot, managed to escape her torturers only to be murdered by a lynch mob when she returned to her own home. It was on 30 January, 1705, that the mob caught her in Pittenween, beat her and dragged her by the ankles to the sea-front. There she was swung from a rope tied between a ship and the shore, stoned, beaten again and finally crushed to death under a door piled with heavy rocks. Then, just to make sure she really was dead, a man drove his horse and cart over her battered corpse several times.

Though all the other accused men and women were eventually freed, and Patrick Morton was exposed for the liar he undoubtedly was, influenced by a fanatical Puritan priest, none of the lynch mob was ever brought to justice.

Round about the middle of the eighteenth century, the now dilapidated Ardvreck Castle, which stands on the A837 on the shores of Loch Assynt, just outside Inchnadamph, was occupied by an elderly dowager with an evil reputation, who caused considerable trouble in the neighbourhood.

Living nearby was a young married couple who for several years had managed to escape the old woman's attention, but all this changed when their first child was born. The Lady of Ardvreck spread a rumour that the wife had been unfaithful to her husband and that the child was not his. Instead of recognizing this for the malicious scandalmongering that it was, the man began to doubt his faithful wife and even threatened to kill their baby. Distressed, the wife wrote to two of her brothers who lived some considerable distance away, and a few days later they both arrived on a visit to protest their sister's innocence. Her stubborn husband, however, refused to be convinced. Then, one of the brothers, seeing it was a waste of time arguing, suggested that they visit the old Lady of Ardvreck and confront her in an effort to uncover the truth.

The next day, husband and wife and the two brothers set out for the castle, which stands on a promontory, partly rising out of the loch between two hills. On their arrival, the old lady treated them with affected graciousness and answered their questions about their sister with apparent frankness. Finally, seeing the wicked old woman was immovable in her slanderous allegations, the younger brother asked if she would have any objection to putting the matter to the proof by calling in a mutual aquaintance. Smilingly, the old lady agreed and the brother bent down on the stone-flagged floor of the hall and began writing on it with his finger, all the time murmuring in some strange language. As he did so, the loch outside became turbulent and a mist rose from it, blotting out the sun in the previously cloudless sky. Then, a tall figure appeared from nowhere and stood against the wall.

The brother then turned to the doubting husband and told him to put his questions to the apparition. Although the man was terrified, his curiosity about his wife was so great that he managed to croak out the question concerning her fidelity. The figure replied that she always had been faithful and always would be.

No sooner had the mysterious figure spoken, than a terrible storm broke over Ardvreck Castle and a huge wave from the loch burst through the windows. The flagstones in the hall heaved beneath their feet.

'He will not leave without someone's soul for payment', the brother told the old lady. 'Whom can you best spare?'

The Lady of Ardvreck, with faltering steps, opened the door of the hall and, at the same time, a little orphan child who skivvied at the castle came running in, frightened by the storm. The old lady pointed at her. The apparition refused, saying it dare not take the child and, at that, another giant wave from the loch swept through the hall, the water swamping the group of terrified people. Out of sheer desperation, the brother pointed to the Lady of Ardvreck and yelled: 'Take her!' The apparition replied in sombre tones that she was already his, but her time wasn't up. He said that he would take one whom the sister would miss more. Then the unearthly visitor vanished and the storm abated as quickly as it had begun. The frightened people left standing in the hall were puzzled; none of their number was missing, and the dreaded stranger had apparently left without payment. However, when they returned home, they discovered that the baby, whose paternity had been the cause of all the trouble, had died at the same moment the mysterious apparition had disappeared from the hall of Ardvreck Castle.

According to local tradition, for several years after these events took place, all the grain that grew in the immediate vicinity of Loch Assynt was black and withered and no fish could be found in the loch. Then Ardvreck Castle was destroyed by a mysterious fire and the evil old Lady of Ardvreck perished in it. After this, nature was said to have resumed its course; the corn grew golden again and the waters of the Loch Assynt teemed with fish once more.

On the island of Vallay in the Outer Hebrides, you may come across a pit which, it is said, cannot be filled in because a witch was once buried alive in it.

She had been accused of stealing milk by magic – a heinous crime in a society where the cow was a more valuable possession than a wife. There were several ways in which the old witch stole the milk. One was for her to transform herself into a hare and then suck the cows dry. Another was to recite spells while 'milking' the iron chains used to hang pots over the fire. She would also carry milk away in a needle, or in seaweed wrapped around her body and, should anyone damage these objects, then the milk would flow out.

Just who this witch was, or how she was detected, no one knows any more, but the hollow pit is still there today as a reminder of her terrible punishment. The local clan chief ordered that she should be buried up to her neck in the gateway to the cattle-fold. There she remained with the cattle passing over her until her skull was crushed.

Perhaps the most remarkable of all the Scottish witch trials, was that of Isobel Gowdie, a young housewife, which took place before the sheriff of Auldearn in 1662.

Isobel seems to have been a young woman with a wonderful imagination. She even confessed to participating in the most bizarre rites, without being persuaded to do so by the use of torture. Indeed, it was her trial which seems to have confirmed most of the popular ideas about witchcraft – covens of thirteen, baptism by the Devil and satanic orgies on lonely hillsides. She quite cheerfully admitted that she and her companions mounted straws and, after rubbing their bodies with a magic potion and reciting the words of a spell, rode them like horses. She said they could transform themselves into cats, hares and jackdaws and once – according to Isobel at least – they were entertained by the 'Queen of Faery' in the heart of the Downey Hills.

The coven at Auldearn, on the A96 east of Nairn and quite close to the appropriately named Macbeth's Hill, had, according to her, murdered the children of the Laird of Park. She said that clay images thrust into the fire had caused the children to die long and lingering deaths. They appear, however, to have been less successful in disposing of the family of the Laird of Lochlay.

In her confession, Isobel claimed the method chosen in this instance was to boil lumps of dog and sheep flesh together for an entire morning, after which the brew was stirred by the Devil himself. The whole concoction was then spread in places where the family was likely to walk, but it seems they failed to pass that way, for they remained in excellent health.

Isobel also claimed to have been given useful hints and recipes by the Fairy Queen, and was on intimate terms with the Devil, whom she described as 'a meikle black man', and whose embraces were rough. History does not record the ultimate fate of Isobel Gowdie, but in all probability she would have been burnt at the stake.

When, in 1562, Mary, Queen of Scots, led her troops into battle against the Earl of Huntley, chief of the Gordon clan, Huntley went cheerfully to war, bolstered by the witches of Strathbogie who told him that after the battle he would lie in the Tolbooth of Aberdeen 'without any wound on his body!'

The armies met on the Hill of Fare, five miles north of Banchory, and the Gordons were defeated. Huntley was captured unwounded but he suddenly fell off his horse, dead from apoplexy. His body, without a wound on it, was taken to the Tolbooth, where it lay for the night and thus fulfilled the witches' prophecy.

As a point of interest, there is a chair-shaped stone on the Hill of Fare, on which Mary, Queen of Scots, is said to have sat to watch the fighting. Just below the slope is a modern memorial commemorating the battle.

John Macgillichallum, Laird of Raasay, was an heroic figure of a man with a fine physique, penetrating mind and a great firmness of character. In particular he was the sworn enemy of all practitioners of the black arts and he had hounded many a witch to her death. Unhappily, this made him a marked man and the constant object of vengeance, so far as the local witches were concerned.

One day, John and a group of friends sailed to Lewis on a deer-hunting trip. They enjoyed a good day at the hunt and afterwards spent a boisterous night on the island, celebrating their fine kill. The following morning, when, with aching heads they went to the boat intending to return to Raasay, they found the sea very turbulent. Some of the more cautious members of the party wanted to wait until the weather abated, but John would not hear of it. However, realizing that some of his companions were suffering from terrible hangovers and needed something to stiffen their resolution, he took them to the ferry house, where they happily consumed several bottles of whisky.

Then an argument broke out over whether or not it was safe to venture out to sea in such weather. While the argument still raged, a wrinkled old woman, bent over a crutch, hobbled into the ferry house. John appealed to her to give an opinion as to whether or not she thought the voyage home would be safe enough. The old woman replied firmly that it was, adding some sneering comments about 'big men afeared of wee waves'. This remark stung the doubters and, bolstered by the whisky, they made a unanimous decision to set sail.

They had not sailed far from land, when they began to realize that sailing conditions were much worse than they had imagined. The effects of the whisky had worn off and seeing they were likely to founder at any moment, they tried to bring the boat about and put back into Lewis, but the wind was against them and it was not possible. On the other hand, it was some consolation to them that the wind was at least carrying them swiftly towards Raasay.

John Macgillichallum took the helm himself, encouraging the crew by his own example. He held the boat firmly on course for Skye, the closest landfall on their homeward route. Meanwhile the weather continued to worsen, with thunder and lightning added to the rough seas and heavy gale. But the coast of Skye was looming up and John seemed to be steering straight and true. At the sight of this, the spirits of the passengers began to revive.

Then, to their amazement, a large cat was seen climbing the rigging. A moment or two later, a second cat appeared and then a third. Those watching now remembered the old woman at the ferry house and a suspicion of her true nature began to dawn on them. Very soon, the masts, shrouds and the entire boat were covered with cats of all descriptions which terrified all on board, for they knew that John Macgillichallum had long been marked for destruction by the witches.

However, John remained unconcerned, doggedly holding the vessel on course. But even he was filled with horror when a huge black cat, larger than the rest, appeared on the mast-head in obvious command of the others. John realized at once what was about to happen, so he launched an attack on the army of cats, but he was too late. With a combined effort, the cats capsized the boat on her leeward side, so that everyone on board was drowned. Thus the witches had avenged themselves on their inveterate enemy, John Macgillichallum, Laird of Raasay.

Readers of a sceptical disposition will now be asking: 'If no one survived, how is it that so much is known of what occurred on the boat that day?' The answer is simple. These details were supplied by the confession of the Goodwife of Laggan, who participated in the murder and who is mentioned in an earlier chapter. It will be recalled that she herself was mortally injured later the same day.

Nanny McMillan was a witch who lived just outside the gates of the manse at Kirkcowan, on the B733 nine miles north-west of Wigton. So notorious was she that even the most stout-hearted locals hurried past her cottage and always treated her with great respect.

There also lived in Kirkcowan at that time, a man who made his living by hunting hares and who had a reputation for bringing down the swiftest of these animals. He plied his trade, which in the eighteenth century was a profitable one, in and around the village and in particular on a part of the land behind the manse which ran down to the River Biadnoch, where the yellow-flowered shrubs and plants gave shelter to many hares. He was also skilled in tracking wounded hares.

According to tradition, there was one large plump hare which he saw quite often but was never able to catch it. Somehow, even bullets seemed not to touch it. Day after day he would watch it at play and day after day, it defied all his crafty efforts. Then one day he put a silver bullet in his pocket, believing it to be infallible against witchery and vampirism.

When at last his chance came to shoot, the large hare rolled head-over-heels into the shrubbery, then it suddenly recovered and made off towards the village, the hunter racing after it. He could see it was bleeding from the head and he knew he had obviously wounded it pretty badly.

At Nanny McMillan's cottage, the hare ran round an angle of the wall and was lost. Despite his skill at tracking, the hare hunter could find no trace of the wounded animal beyond this point. So, summoning up his courage, he knocked on Nanny's door. At first there was no answer, but his continued knocking brought a request to wait a minute. Eventually the door opened a chink and an agitated voice asked what he wanted. The hunter asked, rather nervously, if she had seen a large hare pass her door, to which Nanny replied that she had not. 'Are ye sure?' the hunter urged, at the same time pushing at the door in his eagerness. Then he quickly retreated, for Nanny stood there, her head bound up just above the eye – exactly where his silver bullet had struck the uncanny beast.

Another well-known Scottish witch was Maggie Osborn of Ayr. A woman of extremely strong character, she was the natural daughter of the Warlock Laird of Fail and had been carefully instructed in the black arts by her father. It is said that so many devils and imps attended her midnight excursions into Galloway, no grass will grow to this day on her path over the Carrick Hills, still known as 'Maggie's gate to Galloway'.

One evening as she was out on one of her excursions, Maggie saw a funeral procession approaching and, as some of the mourners had good cause to know her, she thought it prudent to change herself into the form of a beetle. In this form, she was creeping along the side of the road when one of the mourners unwittingly stepped on her. At the time she was in a hollow rut and this saved her, but from that time onwards, she strove with all her arts to ruin the unfortunate man.

Success did not come at once, but one evening the man forgot to say Grace before supper. This was what Maggie was waiting for, his guardian angel had deserted him and Maggie rolled a wreath of snow on his house which killed the whole family, with the exception of one son who was visiting friends in the Hebrides.

But even he was not to escape. When his ship reached the Bay of Ayr, Maggie shut herself in the top room of her house and told her maid to fill a large barrel with water, set an ale-cup floating and await further orders. Three times the maid was sent to report on how things went with the wooden drinking bowl. The first time it was rocking on rippling water; the second time the water was rising over the top of the drinking bowl, dashing it from side to side; the third time there was calm water and the wooden drinking bowl had disappeared.

According to William Robertson in his *Historical Tales of Ayrshire* published in 1889, Maggie Osborn was arrested and tried for this crime and was sentenced to death for witchcraft. As she was being burned at the stake, her last words were addressed to the Devil: 'Oh you fause lad, instead of a black gown you have given me a red one. Have I deserved this for serving you so long?' Then, screaming and writhing in the flames, Maggie Osborn died.

At the northern end of Ben Wyvis, the Allt Graat – or 'Ugly Burn' – flows out of Loch Glass, some six miles from the A9, west of the Cromarty Firth. Along its course to the sea it flows through Glen

Glass in a rushing succession of waterfalls and through a gorge over one hundred feet deep. In places it is overgrown with thick vegetation and many are the animals that have fallen to their deaths at a place called Pol Slugain.

Near Pol Slugain stands the Black Rock, a vast cave which is approachable only by rope from some eighty feet above, and which, so I am told, was a secret whisky still in olden times. It is said that the fumes from the whisky were dispersed by the spray from the falling water, which is why the place was never discovered.

Many years ago a young English nobleman was a guest of a family of similar standing in the area. They held a ball in his honour at Alness, on the A9 between Invergordon and Dingwall. As this was a Highland ball, the young Englishman sat alone for some length of time, watching the dances which were as foreign to him as the 'Lambeth Walk' would have been to the Highlanders. Suddenly, he noticed a beautiful young woman, with raven-black hair and big dark eyes. When the orchestra changed to playing a lilting Austrian waltz, the young man invited the dark-eyed beauty to dance with him.

When the music stopped and they walked from the dance floor, a servant approached the young woman to take her home. The Englishman escorted her to her carriage but before he had time to ask her name, the carriage and its beautiful occupant had disappeared out of sight. It had been love at first sight and, with his curiosity aroused, the young man enquired from his hosts as to the identity of the sad-looking young woman. He was told that she was the Lady of Balconie, a strange, lonely young woman, who loved to walk at night along the banks of the Allt Graat by the Black Rock. The fearful surroundings of this remote place held an uncanny fascination for her. The young Englishman was advised to stay well clear of the area.

But he was young and hot-blooded and so, despite the warnings, he was determined to visit the spot the next night and meet once more the beautiful Lady of Balconie. He reached the Black Rock just as darkness began to fall and here, high above the chasm, they met and embraced in the swirling spume, while around them the night wind howled and far below the waters seethed. As they stood in each others arms, the young woman explained why she was unable to return the Englishman's love.

Some years before, a serious illness had robbed her of her beauty and she had entered into a pact with the Devil that if he would make her beautiful for the next five years, he could have her soul in payment at the end of that period. But once the bargain had been struck, she began to regret it. For five years she had been the most beautiful and the most sought after woman in the whole area, but now the time had come to fulfil her part of the bargain. The five years were up and the Devil would come this very night to claim her soul.

Even as she spoke, a tall sinister figure loomed up through the mist and in a deep commanding voice, called the Lady of Balconie to follow him. The young nobleman felt her slipping from his grasp over the brink of the gorge. With a wild cry of despair, he dived after her into the raging pool below and was dashed to pieces on the jagged rocks.

Local tradition attributes the disappearance of the beautiful Lady of Balconie to the Devil, and they say that he is keeping her a prisoner in the gloomy cave in the Black Rock. For when the mists swirl among the tree-tops over the ravine, the locals say that she is busy at her baking. More tangible are the stories told of how, on moonlit nights when the river is in flood and the wind moans through the gullies, the wistful ghost of the beautiful, raven-haired Lady of Balconie can be seen drifting about the area of the Black Rock, searching for her dashing English nobleman.

For several centuries, Scotland has been renowned for its Seers, or spectral haunted persons who, on occasion, are able to obtain glimpses into another world of sense, as we know it. The 'taibhsear', is not a witch in the true sense of the word, but is a person with a sympathetic sensitivity which enables him or her to prophesy the future.

One of the foremost was the thirteenth-century Scottish prophet, Thomas the Rhymer of Ercildoun, who was said to have foretold the crowning of Robert the Bruce and to have prophesied the Battle of Flodden in 1513. But his best known prophesy was said to have been fulfilled as recently as 1921, when Field Marshal Earl Haig was restored to his family's Bemersyde estates.

Another famous seer was, of course, Michael Scott, who has been mentioned elsewhere in this book. He is said to have flown to France mounted on a demon horse to seek some form of redress for French acts of piracy. In Paris, he made his diabolical steed stamp its hoof and when every steeple bell in the city jangled and part of the palace collapsed, the French king is reported to have hurriedly met Scott's demands.

But of all the Scottish seers, perhaps the best known was Coinneach Odhar – the Brahan Seer, reputed to have lived in several places in the Highlands and Islands, where a man of that name was arrested for witchcraft on the Earl of Seaforth's estate in 1577. His powers were said to have been given to him by the fairies, who presented him with a magic stone. The first thing he discovered on looking into it was that the dinner he was about to eat was poisoned. This revelation obviously preserved him long enough to prophesy the Battle of Culloden, the Highland Clearances and the coming of the railways.

However, this gift of second sight was to prove to be double-edged. Rashly, though as it turned out, accurately, he informed the Countess of Seaforth that the Earl, supposedly away on business, was in fact in the arms of another woman. The Countess had him burned at the stake for his impudence. Before he died, however, he cursed the family and prophesied that the last of the Seaforths would be deaf and dumb, and his sons would die before him. He also said that the inheritor of the estates would be a 'white-hooded lassie who would kill her sister'.

In 1815, Francis Mackenzie, the last of the Seaforth line, died after an illness that made him deaf and dumb. His eldest daughter, wearing white, in mourning for her own husband, inherited the estate. Later, when the daughter was out driving in her carriage – her sister was thrown out and killed!

The prophecies of the Brahan Seer, who was in fact a native of Lewis, are well known and firmly believed by Highlanders to be genuine predictions, uttered by a man with whose name they have been associated for several centuries. In one respect he was different from other seers, due to the fact he made his prophecies by gazing into a crystal ball. By all accounts there have been few instances of this type of divination in the Highlands, where the visions of seers are usually spontaneous and uninvoked.

At the end of the nineteenth century, a crofter living at Edderton, a village on the A9 about 15 miles north of

Invergordon, had a remarkable gift of second sight. He seldom failed to see phantom funeral processions before the death of anyone in the district and was able to say with such accuracy that someone, whom he named, was about to die. So accurate was he, his neighbours shunned him like the plague for fear he might have some calamity to tell them.

One day he was walking along what is the present A9, on his way to Tain, some three or four miles away. He was just about to cross over a bridge, when he 'saw' a funeral cortège coming towards him. Although he recognised it for the ghostly procession it was, he nevertheless felt it prudent to step to one side and let it pass. As it passed him, he received a kick on the leg from a phantom horse ridden by one of the ghostly mourners. Although the cortège was one of phantoms, the blow was real enough and he felt the pain very acutely, forcing him to limp back home.

On arriving home, he told his wife what had taken place, but although she examined his leg thoroughly, she could find no trace of injury such as one would expect from the kick of a horse. But the crofter stuck to his story and went off to bed, still complaining of the severe pain in his leg.

The following morning, the pain was gone and he went about his daily chores as usual. He still had to complete his errand in Tain and later in the day, set off along the same road and over the same bridge where he met a *real* funeral cortège, right at the very same spot that the ghostly procession had passed him the day before. He reverently stepped aside to allow the mourners to pass, when a horse in the procession suddenly shied and kicked him severely on the leg. He limped home as he had done the previous day and his injury was so bad that he was forced to spend several days in bed.

And what about today? Are there still witches and seers to be found in Scotland? Certainly there are still quite a few people in the more remote islands who retain the gift of second sight. Within living memory there was a woman residing on Lewis who was well known for her remarkable predictions, and no event of public importance had happened on the island for several years which she had not foretold in some way.

One incident in particular is still spoken about today when, at a meeting held in the local hall, a Mr Alec Morrison was authorized to take a message of some importance to a Dr Ross who lived some distance away. It is said that before Mr Morrison left the meeting, the old woman turned to a group of people near her and said: 'If Alec Morrison comes back, his horse will not!'

The remarkable and undisputed fact is that as soon as the horse, which Alec Morrison had borrowed from the local horse-hirer, reached the end of its journey it fell down and died.

# 10  Nessie

Ten thousand years ago – give or take a thousand years – the last remaining Ice Age glaciers carved a vast twenty-four mile crevice in the Highlands. As the ice melted, the crevice filled with water and became what we know today as Loch Ness, the home of one of the most mysterious and best-loved phenomena in the whole of Scotland – the Loch Ness Monster.

The monster, known affectionately as Nessie, has, according to legend, haunted the loch ever since the first reported sighting by St Columba in AD 565, when he was travelling to Inverness on a mission to bring Christianity to the Scottish tribes. We are told that he ordered one of his followers to swim out into Loch Ness and bring back a small boat which had drifted from the shore. As the man started out, a strange beast rose from the water a few yards away. St Columba is said to have faced the creature, demanding in a loud voice that it 'Go no further, nor touch the man', at which the monster dived beneath the surface and vanished.

Ever since, the people of the Great Glen have recognised Nessie and her forebears as shy, retiring and harmless creatures who rarely visit the surface of their mountain home. Although the local inhabitants have known about Nessie for centuries, it is only within the last 60 years or so that the monster's fame has spread around the world.

On 14 April, 1933, a local hotel owner and his wife were driving along the newly built road alongside Loch Ness. The smooth water of the loch mirrored the surrounding peaks. Suddenly, his wife clutched his arm in alarm and pointed out across the water. The surface was bubbling and frothing and, as the frightened driver brought the car to a halt, they watched with fearful fascination as a gigantic creature emerged. It had a snakelike neck and at least two humps or coils, and it splashed about in the water making the surface of the loch white with foam. Then suddenly, it dived and disappeared from sight.

Since that day, Nessie has played hide-and-seek with scientists, naturalists and possibly thousands of monster-hunters, and there have been at least 3,000 sightings of the elusive Nessie in the intervening years.

A similar encounter in November of the same year gave the impetus for the Loch Ness Monster cult to start up in earnest, for this time it was to provide the first ever photograph of the shy Nessie.

Local engineer, Hugh Gray, was walking from church to his home in the village of Foyers one bright Sunday morning. Again, the loch was as still and as silent as a mill pond but, 100 yards offshore, Mr Gray noticed a strange disturbance. He later described what he saw as a 'rounded back and tail which suddenly appeared and a creature some 40 foot long began to churn the water, sending up a cloud of spray'.

Mr Gray had the presence of mind to photograph the 'thing' before it disappeared and the resultant print was sent to Kodak for analysis. Kodak confirmed that the film had not been tampered with, but the rather blurred and shadowy image was considered unconvincing evidence of the existence of the Loch Ness Monster.

Perhaps the photograph taken by London doctor, Robert Wilson, a man of unquestioned character, gives the best evidence of Nessie's existence. In April 1934, he and a friend were driving alongside Loch Ness at the start of a holiday during which they hoped to take wildlife photographs. The wildlife pictures Dr Wilson took on that day were of a form he couldn't have imagined in his wildest dreams.

The two men had driven throughout the night and had stopped for a rest and to stretch their legs, near Invermorriston. As Dr Wilson casually strolled beside the loch, he became aware of what seemed to be a small head, peering at him out of the water. He dashed back to the car, grabbed his camera and took a series of photographs, which later showed an elegant neck and head, with the outline of the body remaining beneath the surface.

However, these photographs like the hundreds taken since, were immediately dismissed by the debunkers as showing tree trunks, seals, birds, otters and upturned boats. But whatever the truth, these first reports and pictures claiming to be of the Loch Ness Monster, were to cause a world-wide sensation.

Before very long the loch was crawling with tourists, scientists, schoolboys, hoaxers and even big-game hunters. The circus owner, Bertram Mills, offered £20,000 to anyone who could deliver Nessie to him alive. Local villagers did a roaring trade in bed and breakfasts and questions were asked in Parliament which resulted in the passing of a law forbidding the shooting, trapping or molesting of any creature in the loch.

The one thing lacking, however, was a serious scientific examination of the evidence pouring out of the area each day. One of the main reasons for this seems to have been a series of hoaxes – phoney sightings, touched-up photographs etc – which were rapidly turning the Loch Ness Monster into a huge international joke, the canny Scots having found another way of extracting money from the pockets of gullible foreigners.

One of the earliest hoaxes involved a highly respected Fellow of the Zoological Society, the big-game hunter, Michael Wetherell. In December 1933, he discovered what appeared to be the monster's footprint on the shore of the loch, which he claimed was a 'four-legged beast with feet or pads some eight inches across and estimated to be a most powerful animal, some twenty foot long'.

Amid much publicity and mounting excitement, plaster casts of the footprint were sent to the Natural History Museum in London where they were examined by experts. They announced with due solemnity that the print resembled that of a hippopotamus – and their faces must have been very red indeed, when it was later discovered that a dried and mounted hippo's foot had been stolen from the museum at Inverness a few miles away.

Of the three most sensational sightings reported in 1933 and 1934, two were by local people and the third was by London company director, George Spicer, who told a fantastic story of his encounter with the monster. He told how he and his wife were driving along the new road alongside the loch, when they both saw an extraordinary animal, with a long neck and large body, crossing the road about 200 yards ahead of them. He said it had a dark, loathsome skin and moved with a jerky motion, disappearing into the thick undergrowth.

On a June day in 1934, local journalist, Alexander Campbell, saw the monster as he left his cottage close by Loch Ness. He described it as about 30 foot long, with a snakelike neck and a flat tail. At the joint of the neck and body there was a hump. Campbell said that the creature was basking in the sunshine but the sound of a boat from the Caledonian Canal disturbed it. Suddenly Nessie lowered his neck and dived, leaving a minor tidal wave behind it.

The third sighting was by a monk, Brother Horan, of St Benedict's Abbey at Fort Augustus. He claimed to have seen the monster rise out of the waters of the loch and he watched it for nearly half an hour. Again, when Nessie was disturbed by a motor-boat, he disappeared from sight.

Other monster-hunters reported seeing the beast open and close its mouth. Some said it had a mane similar to that of a horse, and one 'spotter' claimed to have seen it close enough to watch drops of water falling from the scaly skin as the monster shook itself.

By the late summer of 1934, Nessie's fame had spread across the Atlantic bringing some good old American know-how on to the scene in the person of John Williamson, a leading expert of the day in underwater photography. He arrived accompanied by all the ballyhoo which only the Americans know how to generate and bringing with him a contraption which he called his 'photosphere', a submersible, windowed globe, in which he sat in a plush armchair to take underwater photographs.

Of course, what Williamson did not know, was that below about 30 feet, the water is first dark brown, then inky black and even his most powerful lights could not penetrate more than a couple of feet. This murkiness is caused by particles of peat which have been washed down from the mountains and into Loch Ness for many thousands of years. A chagrined Williamson had to abandon his plans and hurried back home.

Each year up until the outbreak of World War II, scores of sightings were reported and many more photographs were taken. But during the war there were no tourists as the roads around Loch Ness were used only by the locals and by the Armed Forces. Nessie was overtaken by world events and stopped making the news.

It was 1947 before the Loch Ness Monster hit the front pages again. In that year, the clerk to Inverness County Council and a group of friends reported seeing the humps of a large beast swimming across the loch. Once more the monster-hunting season had got underway.

In 1951, Lachlan Stuart, a local forester, rose early and stepped out of the door of his croft. He glanced across towards the loch and stopped in his tracks, before dashing back inside to pick up his camera. He ran down to the shoreline and managed to take just one photograph before his shutter jammed, but that one photograph revealed three humps sticking some three to four feet out of the water. Stuart estimated the creature to be some fifty to sixty feet long.

Throughout the 1950s several sightings were recorded, but it was not until 1960 that Nessie was recorded on movie film for the very first time. It was a four-minute sequence taken by aviation engineer, Tim Dinsdale. This clearly showed a humpbacked creature zig-zagging through the water at approximately ten miles an hour. Dinsdale was so convinced by what he had filmed, he gave up a good career to live by the loch and hunt for the monster.

In 1962, world famous naturalist, Sir Peter Scott, helped launch the Loch Ness Phenomena Investigation Bureau, to organise a serious study of the mystery. For ten years, Bureau volunteers and a few full-time workers kept a constant watch on the loch, their cameras ready round the clock. They were to log many sightings of their own and put on record scores of eyewitness accounts. Unfortunately, the only prize worth having for such an effort was to elude them, and they too failed to obtain a definitive photograph of the Loch Ness Monster.

One of the most useful things the Bureau did, was to send films of what was claimed to be Nessie to the Joint Air Reconnaissance Intelligence Centre for independent analysis. The centre reported that one film showed an object which was neither a boat nor a submarine, but which appeared to be 'an animate object', twelve to fifteen feet long, three foot high and six foot wide. Another film showed a similar object.

But the greatest chance the Loch Ness Phenomena Investigation Bureau had of solving the mystery, was blown in 1971. Tim Dinsdale was directing a 100-strong team of investigators, when a black, snakelike headed creature suddenly reared out of the water. Dinsdale had at least half a dozen cameras, but was too astonished to use any of them!

In 1969, Cockney ex-paratrooper, Frank Searle, gave up his job as a grocery store manager, spent a small fortune on first-rate photographic equipment and went to live in a tent by Loch Ness. One more in an ever-growing band of Nessie fanatics to take up monster-hunting as a profession.

Searle spent weeks sitting, watching and waiting for his chance to make a fortune. He reckoned that it would only be a matter of time before his patience was rewarded and he would obtain the first totally convincing pictures of Nessie, which could be worth £250,000 in worldwide publication fees.

He claims to have seen more than one monster, estimating that there is a colony of at least twenty of them, which he has seen on many occasions. He says: 'They're bulky, twelve to sixteen feet long, with sheep-like heads and necks about seven foot long. They have paddle-like flippers.'

In 1971 and again in 1976, Searle took photographs which he claims were of the monsters. Indeed, they were published worldwide and described as 'the most amazing yet'. But a Professor of Zoology at Glasgow University was to debunk them as 'the carcass of an animal which has been in the water for some time'.

By the late 1970s, monster-hunting had become a major British sport and Nessie became the Scottish Tourist Board's biggest single asset. Various ways of cornering or enticing the monster were suggested. Dragging the loch with steel nets was ruled out, after the estimated cost came to over £200,000. So was a scheme to induce Nessie to bask in water warmed by giant hot-plates sunk into the loch. Tests with a British miniature submarine, some 450 feet below the surface proved disappointing. It was so thick and black down there, the occupants could see absolutely nothing.

The Americans invaded the area in 1969. Don Taylor, a former US Navy submariner from Atlanta, Georgia, had spent five years and over £20,000 in building a tiny yellow glass-fibre submarine which he named 'Viperfish'. He planned to fire darts from it to remove a sliver of 'Nessie's flesh. Taylor claimed to have picked up echoes of the monster on his sonar, but never for long enough to track it.

Unfortunately for him, he had repeated John Williamson's mistake of 35 years earlier, and had not realised how impenetrable the waters of the loch are below the depth of 30 feet. He too packed up and went home.

Then in 1970, Dr Robert Rines, president of the Academy of Applied Science in Massachusetts, spent two weeks at Loch Ness. He headed a four-man team equipped with sonar gear, underwater cameras and a 'sex cocktail', made from the reproductive essences of creatures such as sea-cows, eels and sea-lions. The team also had tapes, to be played underwater, of the sounds made by a variety of creatures mating, fighting and 'talking'.

Dr Rines later claimed that the so-called 'sex cocktail' had enabled him to make contact with creatures 'one hundred times the size of any fish in the loch'. They lived, he said, on a shelf 200 feet from the shore. Two years later, Rines produced in Boston, colour and black-and-white photographs which he said were taken in the loch and which he also claimed showed a very large flipper attached to a cow-shaped body.

Round about the same time as Dr Rines' expedition, another US team arrived at the loch. This one, sponsored by the Cutty Sark whisky manufacturers, was led by Professor James Ullrich of the Smithsonian Institute. Cutty Sark had offered £1 million to anyone who caught Nessie alive and unharmed, before May 1972. There were no serious claims and Ullrich's team, using more or less the same methods as Dr Rines, failed to get any better evidence than its predecessors to support or crack the legend.

Next to jump on the Nessie bandwaggon were the Japanese. Yoshiou Kou, the Japanese showman responsible for bringing such people as Tom Jones and Muhammad Ali to Japan, led a fifteen-man team to the shores of Loch Ness. A Tokyo business consortium had raised the cash, and Kou announced that his team would use two submarines to solve the legend of Nessie once and for all. But again, when his divers saw how inky-black the water of the loch was, they refused to go down and the mission had to be cancelled.

Meanwhile, the amateurs seemed to be having more success. In 1974, Nessie was spotted by a truck driver and his mate, and the following year, two German students claimed to have seen several humps moving around in the water. Ten days later, four French girls reported a similar sighting and their reports were supported by a group of English tourists.

Yet still there was no convincing evidence. Perhaps the most convincing photographic evidence came as a result of a second attempt at capturing the monster on film by Dr Rines in June 1975. His team lowered two underwater cameras into the loch near Urquhart Castle to depths of forty and eighty feet. They took over 2,000 photographs at 75-second intervals, aided by immensely powerful strobe lights. This time they appear to have been more successful and the resulting photographs seemed to depict a reddish-brown beast with a fat body. It was about twelve foot long with an arching neck a further eight-foot long. The creature had a hideous head, with gaping jaws and two tube-like protuberances on top of it.

These photographs convinced Sir Peter Scott, at least, that Nessie was no figment of the imagination and he really existed. He was later to state publicly that there are probably between twenty and fifty creatures in the loch, all of which are related to the plesiosaurs.

The plesiosaur has not been seen on earth for seven million years. The monster-hunters believe that Nessie's ancestors may have been cut off from the sea when the loch was formed at the end of the last Ice Age. Loch Ness is up to 1,000 feet deep – deeper than the North Sea – and its vastness and remoteness would have allowed the creatures to flourish undisturbed as survivors from another millennium. But why the spate of sightings from 1933 onwards?

The monster-hunters have an explanation for that too. The road that the local hotel owner and his wife were driving along when they first spotted Nessie in April 1933, had only just been built and was the first to skirt the loch. In order to construct it, thousands of tons of rock had been blasted into Loch Ness, and dense vegetation, which for centuries had shrouded its banks, had been cut down. This blasting, they argue, destroyed the monster's primeval underwater lairs and left them, for the very first time, homeless wanderers in the loch.

There seems to be an attitude among many biologists that if one is not able to dissect something in a laboratory, then it is not worth giving serious consideration. Hard-line opponents of the possibility of an unknown air-breathing animal like a plesiosaur, somehow living millions of years beyond its time, note the absence of a dead specimen with an 'I think you prove the crime when you have the corpse' attitude.

This problem certainly applies in the case of the Loch Ness Monster, and with the absence of evidence – concrete evidence

– many scientists and biologists will, perhaps understandably, continue to reject the monster idea. Yet the Belgian zoologist, Bernard Heuvelmans, has shown that it is totally unscientific to dismiss reports just because they do not coincide with the known catalogue of the world's sea-creatures.

He found it relatively easy to sort out the deliberate hoaxes and the mistakes, from the 500 or more reports of monster-sightings he examined, which dated from 1639 to 1964. Even after eliminating these, and the ones too vague to be useful, he was still left with 350 which he had no reason to doubt.

Such reports have a ring of truth about them and after a full and careful analysis which took in such details as location of sighting, general shape, length, relative size of head, neck, limbs, appearance of skin, method of propulsion, speed, behaviour, and many more characteristics, nine specific types of underwater monster emerged, although many are beyond the scope of this chapter.

This then, suggests that Nessie is not the only monster living in Scottish waters. Indeed, over the years there have been numerous reported sightings of these creatures all around the Scottish coast as well as in other lochs.

In 1857, Lord Malmesbury was told by his stalker of a 'monster' he had seen in Loch Arkaig, but when he proposed to go and shoot it the stalker said: 'Perhaps your Lordship's gun would misfire!'

The Times reported in March 1856, that the village of Leurbost on the Island of Lewis was the scene of some unusual activity, when an animal 'of great size and dimension' put in an appearance in one of the inland freshwater lochs, and which puzzled the naturalists. Some supposed this to be a description of the hitherto mythological water-kelpie, while others said it appeared to be the description of a sea-serpent.

For a period of two weeks this 'monster' was repeatedly seen by crowds of people, many of whom had come from the remotest parts of the island to witness for themselves the uncommon spectacle. The animal was described by some as being about the size of a huge peat stack, while others claimed that 'a six-oared boat could pass between the huge humps which were occasionally visible'. All however, agreed in describing its form as like that of a monster eel, about forty feet in length. The creature reportedly swallowed a blanket left on the bank of the loch by a girl herding cattle!

According to Bernard Heuvelmans, there have been thirty-three sightings of this many-humped sea-serpent, whose size has been estimated at between sixty and one hundred feet. He says the creature is almost exclusive to the warm waters of the North Atlantic Gulf Stream. It has a caterpillar-like motion at twenty to forty knots and the humps may be air-filled sacs to allow for prolonged diving. He does not, however, offer any suggestion as to how the creature could have got into the land-locked freshwater loch.

A number of merhorses have reportedly been seen around European coastal waters – three sightings being reported off Cape Wrath. These mammals, up to ninety feet in length, live mostly at about 100 fathoms depth and are said to be fast enough to catch and eat squid. The long-necked super-eel has also been spotted at least a dozen times off the northern tip of Scotland. It has even been observed fighting sperm whales.

So what are we to make of Nessie and his relatives? Despite intensive and expensive efforts, nobody has yet succeeded in luring one of these monsters into a position where it can be conclusively photographed, or trapped long enough for an examination to be made. After Dr Rines had secured his blurred 1975 underwater photographs from which, after computer enhancement, Sir Peter Scott was able to paint a plausible reconstruction of the creature, the National Geographical Society mounted an expedition in an attempt to verify its existence.

An ingenious sonar bait was used, transmitting underwater the simulated sound pattern made by the movement of a wounded fish. The device was tested off the coast of Florida and within minutes had been viciously attacked by shoals of sharks from several *miles* away. Yet, when it was tried later that same summer in Loch Ness, Nessie stubbornly refused to be tempted!

So whatever the monster feeds on, it is unlikely to be the local salmon, and this is the first of the many paradoxes that surround the creature. Nobody can doubt for one minute that *something* has been seen and photographed many times with some success. That every sighting is a hoax or self-delusion simply doesn't stand up to investigation. A few years ago researchers for an American TV series, interviewed more than twenty witnesses who had not only vivid and consistent stories to tell, but who simply had no overt reason for inventing them. Doctors, policemen, retired people who actively dislike the crowds Nessie brings, were only representative of a tiny fraction of the possible thousands, who have seen an unusual object in the loch since the road alongside opened in 1933, making 'Nessie' sightings all that much easier.

But at the same time, whatever is there has much in common with ghosts and UFOs so long as hard evidence remains defiantly elusive. Perhaps if it was defined as a UMO (Unidentified Moving Object), it would be more appropriate. No carcass has ever been found, although the reason for this could well be that the nature of the cold, steep-sided loch causes them to sink to the bottom. No obvious food source is known; cameras and photographs have a strange habit of jamming or fogging at the crucial moment. It is, in fact rather disturbing when one realises that hardly any of the original negatives of the better known Loch Ness Monster photographs taken since 1933 have survived. Nessie photographs are somehow supernaturally prone to accidents.

There are many references in old histories to the same water-monsters that are seen today, and they are always represented as being different from ordinary creatures, elemental rather than faunal. Sea-serpents, however exaggerated some tales of the past might be, are a reality, and Nessie may yet turn out to be a reality too.

# Index

# Index